THE LITTLE GENERAL

A Legacy of Resilience:
The Story of a Holocaust Survivor and His Unbreakable Spirit

ROBERT "BOLEK" BECKER

ABSOLUTE AUTHOR PUBLISHING HOUSE

Publisher: Absolute Author Publishing House
Editor: Dr. Melissa Caudle

Paperback ISBN: 978-1-64953-994-6
Hardback ISBN: 978-1-64953-995-3
eBook ISBN: 978-1-64953-996-0
ISBN: 978-1-64953-997-7

1. Memoir   2. Biography   3. Historical Account

PRINTED IN THE UNITED STATES OF AMERICA

TABLE OF CONTENTS

FOREWORD By Liz Becker v

CHAPTER 1: The Interruption of Everything 1

CHAPTER 2: Survival 8

CHAPTER 3: Working Day and Night 14

CHAPTER 4: Underground 21

CHAPTER 5: Fight or Flight 27

CHAPTER 6: Love and Loss 33

CHAPTER 7: According to Plan 39

CHAPTER 8: The Unimaginable 44

CHAPTER 9: Back in Action 48

CHAPTER 10: Behind Enemy Lines 54

CHAPTER 11: New Orders 61

CHAPTER 12: On My Own 66

CHAPTER 13: Full Circle 72

CHAPTER 14: No End in Sight 78

CHAPTER 15: Journey to Liberty 85

CHAPTER 16: A Different Course 91

CHAPTER 17: Changes on the Horizon 96

CHAPTER 18: New Beginnings 101

CHAPTER 19: To the Rescue 108

CHAPTER 20: The Next Chapter 113

AFTERWORD By Liz Becker 118

BECKER JUST BEFORE THE WAR STARTED

BECKER 2011

FOREWORD

By Liz Becker

I was privileged growing up in a middle-class family in Toronto, Ontario. I lived in a stable home with two loving parents and two dogs. My half-sister and brother, Sheba and Harvey, from my father's previous marriage, lived in the United States. Even though there was a large gap in age, and we did not grow up in the same house, I saw them often, and they were a very important part of my life.

I attended a private Jewish school that provided an excellent education and helped me develop a strong sense of community and connection with Israel and the Jewish people. I was a social butterfly and heavily involved in my school and community. Although I never lacked friends and always felt like I fit in no matter who I was with, there was always something different about me. Whether I was in kindergarten, middle school, high school, or college, I was always the only one that had a parent who was a Holocaust survivor. Many of my friends had grandparents who survived, but not parents. My father was significantly older and more unique in many ways compared to other fathers.

It wasn't just his tragic past that set him apart from others. To start, his presence was unquestionably commanding. Whether it was his cowboy attire (hat and all), his endearing smile, or his often-embarrassing sense of humor, everyone was drawn to him. When Bob Becker talked, everyone listened. Luckily, my father could openly talk about his experiences during the war without hesitation or resistance. Hearing his stories regularly helped me understand him better and enlightened me in a way none of my friends could possibly experience. My father's ability to express himself, and not be a victim of his traumatic and torturous past, helped me grow up with an intense sense of optimism and resilience. Having my father's history always present in my mind resulted in my perpetual appreciation for everything I have. No matter my challenge, I grew up believing that in my lifetime, I would never experience the depth of trauma, pain, loss, and fight for survival that my father did, so everything was tolerable.

Upon arriving to the U.S after the war, as recommended by a psychologist he was seeing, my father began to record his experience. Word after word, sentence after sentence, he put his memories down on paper. What was originally intended to be a therapeutic exercise to help him cope with his tragic and horror-filled pass, ultimately culminated into this action-filled collection of stories of survival and resistance- The Little General. Albeit a little rough around the edges, a bit disorganized chronologically, and missing a few names and dates, I am so grateful that he memorialized his past.

For years, it has been my dream to publish my father's story of undeniable strength, determination, and courage so that it may serve as inspiration to all. In my effort to preserve the book's original representation, I carefully edited it without any embellishment. With the heightened antisemitism surfacing throughout the world, now more than ever, we must continue to educate and elicit awareness about the Holocaust so that the memories of all of those fallen will remain alive. With great honor and pride, I share my father's heroic journey, filled with moments of unimaginable tragedy and relentless hope.

As I write these final words, I can see him looking down upon me from above, with a shot of Vodka in his hand and a big grin on his face, and hear his deep voice boldly state the words, "L'chaim" (to life)

BECKER'S FAMILY

TOP ROW FORM LEFT TO RIGHT: Hershel Bekierman (father), Luzer Bekierman (brother), Robert "Bolek" Becker (Bekierman), Sheva Bekierman (mother), Pesl Bekierman (sister)

BOTTOM ROW FROM LEFT TO RIGHT: Joesph Glincman (maternal uncle), Tila Glincman (maternal aunt), Srulke Glincman (maternal uncle)

CHAPTER 1:

The Interruption of Everything

In 1939, when I was close to 15 years old, I lived in a little town on the river Bug called Wlodawa, which separated middle Poland from White Russia. I had lived there since I was born. I was just becoming interested in school. Until then, I loved playing soldiers and similar things like every other young boy. I can still remember playing at the town's surrounding lakes every day after school or on Sundays, where I fished or took long walks breathing in the fresh air that came across from the other side of the river Bug. The name Bug sounds just like Polish word for God, which is "Bog.". I remember enjoying afternoon walks along the river, watching the water flow consistently in the same direction, wishing I could be a fish and jump into the water and swim along with the current to a land somewhere—a land where I could enjoy freedom just like people in other parts of the world.

Those fond memories were quickly tarnished by what happened next: the big German invasion, the so-called Blitz Krieg. Only then did I realize what I had been privileged to experience in such a beautiful and peaceful town as ours. I can recall seeing the first German airplanes and then the first German soldiers. Initially, it was not too bad; however, there was an immediate food shortage. As I had always been a brave boy, I immediately began hanging around the German soldiers and begging for any leftover food and cigarettes. This is how I began to help my family a lot, but in a short time, the German Gestapo came.

1

The first action the Gestapo took was ordering all the Jewish people to gather in the Marketplace. The Gestapo then searched house by house to check if anyone stayed home. Whoever was found in their homes was shot instantly. In the Marketplace, the Gestapo ordered the Jews to form several lines. One line comprised small children between one day and ten years old. They loaded all the children on horse-pulled wagons driven by Gentiles who were forced to do so. The children were driven away and never seen again. Out of the second line, they picked all the females ten years and older who appeared to be healthy and shipped the weak and the sick off, just like the small children. They repeated this process with the male Jews.

At this point, the families were all torn apart, and everyone knew that the chances they would reunite with their loved ones who were sick, malnourished, or simply weak was close to nothing. The Gestapo continued to pick about two hundred people, including myself, and marched us away. Until we arrived at a place about thirty kilometers away from our hometown, we had no idea where they were taking us. We all thought that they were leading us to the same place where they had taken the sick and the children and that this was the end of our lives. After walking all night and day without food or water, we came close to a small place known to most of us as Hansk. We were immediately put to work to build a camp and string up barbed wire, but no buildings or any other kind of shelter were provided. After a week of no food or water, people became sick. I, however, had started from the first day by picking things from the ground, anything I could digest, and drinking water anywhere I found it. That is how I stayed in good shape. After one week, half of the people died from exposure, starvation, and dehydration. Two months passed, and I knew that eventually, everyone there would die, so I knew I had to get out of there as soon as possible, especially because I wanted to find out about the fate of my family that I had left behind at home. I decided to run away.

I called a few of my school friends who had always trusted me and considered me a hero. Twelve of us made a run for it that same night.

2

Among this group, I had three close friends who attended school with me, and when we played soldiers, I was always their commander. Because of their support, it was easy for me to plan the escape. When we broke out of camp around three o'clock the next morning, we were shot at as we had expected. Six were killed, and the remaining six of us ran for our lives into the forest and continued to run until we were deep in the brush. As we were too exhausted to continue, I decided we should rest and made sure we took turns to stand on the lookout.

We slept for twenty-four hours. I was the first to wake up. I saw an old man watching us who appeared to be a nearby farmer. When I looked up, he said a prayer that I could not understand, and he told me not to be afraid and that he lived at the edge of the forest. He invited us to stay in his barn for as long as we liked. It was already getting cold outside, and we were shivering because we were wet and our clothes were all torn from the wear and tear of not having taken them off for over two months, so we graciously accepted his offer. We stayed with the farmer for about two weeks and regained our strength.

Next, I decided it was time to find out what happened to our families. In the early morning hours, we set out for Wlodawa. By daybreak the next morning, we arrived at our hometown and were shocked at what we saw. How strange everything looked! We first noticed a high fence surrounding the town center where most Jewish people lived. There were gates with German soldiers posted at the entrance. We couldn't walk up to the gate and go through, so we split up into groups of two. My cousin Joe and I walked along the fence until we came to a part that was not guarded. We then jumped over the fence and entered the now-called Ghetto, the part of the town surrounded by the fence. We had to be cautious not to be noticed by anyone, so we hid in an old chicken coop and waited. At around six o'clock the following morning, people came out of their houses and walked to the center of the Ghetto, where they formed long lines holding pots in their hands. Soon, we heard the German guards screaming and shouting, and this went on for about an hour. From our hiding place, we watched the people going by and tried to recognize faces, but it was impossible because everyone looked different. Most of the faces we could spot did not look familiar to us. A little later, it became so quiet that it was as though the Ghetto had become deserted. We left the chicken coop and walked the streets, looking into the uninhabited houses.

The entire group met again at my friend Jack's cousin's house. Jack told us he was able to talk to his cousin before she had to leave for work with the others.

All the Jewish people were working on a big German project to dry out the swamps and lakes, the same ones I had enjoyed so much throughout my childhood. Their labor was compensated with merely one hundred grams of bread, a kilo of potatoes, some salt, a bit of oil, and a few vegetables each day. Jack's cousin told him that my family was still alive, but the Germans had taken Joe and Jack's families away a few weeks ago, right after the German authorities heard about our escape from the labor camp in Hansk. He told me where my family lived now, on the other side of town. We waited until dark before traveling there. People started returning from work as evening arrived, so we had to hide. When Jack's cousin arrived home, she shared what little food she had with us. As soon as it became dark and quiet, we headed out to find my parents. Jack's cousin led the way and served as our lookout. At every street corner, she checked first to see if it was all right for us to advance until we finally arrived at my family's house.

I peeked through the window and looked into the dimly lit room. The candlelight shined on my six-foot father, Hershel, my beautiful mother, Sheva, whom I admired so much and always wished I had a girlfriend who looked like her, my little sister Pesa, and my brother Luzer. I could also make out my grandfather and grandmother, whom I loved dearly. They had lived with us for as long as I could remember, and I was willing to give my life for them. Suddenly, I felt paralyzed when I remembered that I had the best grandmother in the world. I could not move and started to cry. It was then I realized that I was still only a little boy. It was 1940, and I was only 15 years old. At that moment, I truly felt like a child.

In the meantime, my friends were standing on the corner on the lookout for anyone approaching in the dark. After I regained my composure, I knocked softly on the window. My father walked outside but could not see me, so I called, "Father, it's me, your son, Bolek." He saw me, grabbed me in his arms, and held me so tightly that if it had lasted a second longer, he would have choked me. He immediately took me inside and asked me many questions: How did I get back? Did anybody see me? I told him, in short, everything that had happened since I saw him last. He asked me to wait a little longer at the house's entrance because he wanted to tell everyone about my arrival first and to caution them not to make any commotion whatsoever to arouse any suspicion from the neighbors.

My father returned and asked us all, including Joe, Jack, and his cousin, to come into the house. Everyone began to cry. It was like Yom Kippur (the Day of Atonement, recognized as the holiest day of the Jewish year). I walked up to my mother and asked her why she was crying, being that I was still alive. They all told me that they had heard of our escape from the labor camp, and the Gestapo was watching our house. I wanted to get out of the house immediately because there was no way I would risk the lives of my beloved family; however, my entire family insisted on us staying overnight. We all warmed up in the house and changed clothes. My mother made us a good meal. She could do this because my father, who was in the construction business, had built homes for the Germans so he could go to work without guards, which enabled him to pick up some extra food from friendly and giving people.

The next day, my father went to the Jewish leader of the Ghetto and told him the entire story. They forged documents for us all so we could register for work. They sent us to work for him because my father could apply for help. Even though we had stayed in the town to work, we could not stay at my parents' house because the Gestapo was still looking for us. We

5

lived like this for about a year and experienced several raids. When least expected, the Gestapo would break into homes, pick up everyone they could find, and send them to concentration camps. Anyone who tried to escape was shot instantly. After every raid, we would come out of hiding and go about our work just like before. We were working for a different German outfit, but for the Gestapo to make their quota, they came over there and stole the Jews from them. It was like a wild goose chase.

In the same Ghetto, some people owned horses. Because everyone had to work, so did the horses. One day, my father received a sick horse from the German army as payment. My father had this horse for about six months and nurtured it to a healthy state. Our town was near the Russian border. The borderline was the river Bug. In 1939, the Germans split Poland with Russia, making the river Bug the demarcation line. German Poland lay on one side of the river, with Russia on the other. One day, at the end of 1940, the Germans debarked a trainload of Jewish POWs (prisoners of war) from the Polish army, whose homes were on the other side of the river Bug in Russia and told them to walk across the frozen river to their homes. When they started to cross the river, the German SS opened fire, killing them all.

As Jewish people believe that every man deserves a proper burial, the leader of the Ghetto ordered the people who owned horses to pick up the dead bodies and bring them back to the cemetery for a religious burial. My father was obligated to go out because he had a horse, but I thought it would be better for me to go, being that it was a considerable risk for a Jew to leave the Ghetto. The Ghetto provided a little protection because no single German would enter the Ghetto to kill a few Jews simply for fun; however, that happened every day outside the Ghetto. If an SS soldier came across a small group of Jews, he killed them mercilessly simply for the thrill it provided him. That is precisely why I decided to go instead of my father. He still had to take care of the entire family.

It was a beautiful day in December, full of snow and sunshine, when I joined the others on my father's horse and sled. I fell behind because I was the youngest among those men, and my horse was the weakest among their horses. Darkness set in when I reached the river to pick up my load. By the time I dragged three bodies on to my sled, it had become completely dark, and had to ride back to town alone. I arrived in town with my frightening load close to midnight. Everything looked so strange in the dark, and I was terrified when I reached the cemetery. I was about to drive through the gate when I realized that I was the only one there. All the others had arrived at the cemetery before me, unloaded their bodies, and piled them up like bricks. I was petrified. I dropped the reins and started to run back to town, but as soon as my horse noticed I had left, it, too, turned and started chasing after me with the three dead bodies still on the sled.

The faster I ran, the faster the horse ran. I screamed so loud that people nearby heard me and came to help. By the time they reached me, I had fallen unconscious. I had passed out from the utter fear. Once I regained consciousness and composed myself, I realized I had envisioned the bodies returning to life and chasing me. After this incident, I was back in the Ghetto, working with my father and friends just as before. Life was going on, but no one knew how long it would last.

CHAPTER 2:

Survival

At the beginning of 1941 came another order from the Gestapo that one hundred Jewish men would have to go to work near our town in a small place called Sobibor. As before, my father was chosen to be one of them. Again, I decided I should go in his place, and so I did. I always was a skinny boy but never lazy. In this camp, we were placed in barracks, like animals, with little food and had to work twelve hours a day. We worked in the forest cutting timber and loaded it by hand onto wagons. Because everyone was undernourished, people tried to grab the thinner end of the timber. It did not matter to me which end of the timber I received because it was all too heavy, so I always tried to lift the thicker end. One day, an SS guard noticed this, pitied me, and called me over. He told me to sit down and that I was a good Jew and should rest and let the other lazy Jews work.

One rainy day, when everything was soaking wet and covered in mud, I noticed that the boots of the SS guard were filthy. I stepped out of a line and attempted to clean his boot with my shirt. The SS guard thanked me with such a hard kick that I almost fainted. I could not sleep at night. Not just because we were on bare floors in the barracks but because I could not stop thinking about my dear family. One night, an SS guard came in and asked for volunteers to bury bodies. There were always bodies to be buried. Everybody was tired, hungry, and cold, so no one responded. I was the only one who got up and answered. The SS guard became angry. He called me over again to tell me that I should go to sleep and let the others

8

get up, and then he ordered all the others out into the night to do the work.

One morning, the SS guard whose boots I had cleaned with my shirt gave me his filthy boots, ordered me to clean them in ten minutes, and told me they should shine like a mirror. I did not have the proper supplies to do so. I was certain that if I did not do what was asked, I would be the next one to be shot. In my desperation, I took a bit of coal from the stove.

Mixing the coal and some water, I polished his boots perfectly. That is when my luck started to change. From that point forward, it was my responsibility to polish the boots of all the SS guards. Gradually they all liked me, and this job practically saved my life.

Instead of going to work, I would stay in camp all day long. I looked everywhere for something to eat, a little more food to give others. Whenever I cleaned a pair of boots, I received a piece of bread or some other edible remainder. This helped me maintain my strength and help others. One day, I was promoted to caretaker of the German police dogs. Despite the danger, those dogs were vicious and could tear a man apart in a second, I was very happy about having that job. It was, however, torture, as their food was the best, but I could not touch it for myself. If an SS soldier had caught me eating the dog food, I would have been a dead duck. Finally, it came to the point that I did not care what would happen to me because I was starving. I had always grabbed what I could get my hands on, so I was not about to stop now. Every time I stole a piece of meat from the dogs, the dogs attacked me. As time passed, the dogs got accustomed to me and became friendly. In fact, they obeyed me as much as they did the SS guards. At this point, I had all the food I needed and built my strength day by day. All the SS guards grew fond of me, which gave me the advantage of walking around the camp without any restriction.

At about the same time we arrived at the camp, work had started on a building, which later turned out to be a crematorium. One day, after this crematorium was completed, a train arrived with ten thousand Jewish people from Poland, Hungary, Romania, and Czechoslovakia. We all were called out and lined up with the new arrivals. After the SS guards had picked out an equal number of young and healthy people to replace us, I realized this would be the end for me.

Sobibor was about the size of three city blocks, surrounded by barbed wire and electric fences with many trees inside and around the camp. In the middle of the camp was a brick building about one hundred by one hundred meters, with no windows and only one metal door.

From the center of the camp to this door ran a narrow walkway bordered by barbed wire, just wide enough for one person to walk through. Fixtures similar to showerheads hung from the ceilings inside. The floor was made of steel and reversible. Underneath the building was a huge ditch, very deep, in the form of a canal extending about one block beyond the building. A structure similar to a catwalk and a small railroad with little freight cars extended from the building.

The SS guards surrounded us as they yelled out orders. First, we all had to undress. Men, women, and children had to drop their clothes in the same place simultaneously. We then had to pass by a place where people had to leave their eyeglasses. At the next stop, everyone had to give up their jewelry, and following that, all the women were shorn of their hair. Finally, everyone received a piece of soap, and we were told we would have to shower. From the beginning of this procedure, we were lined up in a single file that kept moving toward the strange building in the center of the camp. The steel door closed automatically after the first group of about thirty people entered the building. At the time, we did not know, but as soon as the door closed, gas flowed out of the so-called showerheads. Within five minutes, everyone inside was dead. Once it was confirmed that all were dead, the reversible floor would turn over, drop all the bodies into the small wagons on the trains, which would pull out to the end of the canal, and there, the dead bodies were dropped onto piles. When the day was over, they set these piles of Jewish bodies on fire until nothing was left but ashes. Every night, you could see this fire burning from twenty miles away.

After the gas house had been filled three or four times, people wondered what was happening inside. Everyone could see no other door in that building, and no one was coming out again. Once everyone realized what was going on, a terrible cry started. Such a cry I had never heard before or ever since. It sounded like the entire world was in agony; every man, woman, and child cried but continued moving forward in the same line because no one could break out as the SS guards and their dogs watched them closely. If anyone just made the slightest of moves, the guards shot them instantly, and the dogs tore them to pieces.

All this crying, shouting, shooting, barking, and movement continued until I was next to enter the building, knowing this would be the end of my life.

All the time I had stood and moved in this line, I could not think of anything to get me out of there. I was paralyzed or hypnotized as though I were in a trance until I reached the door, and suddenly, it was like a wake-up call. I looked backward and never again looked forward in the direction of this terrifying door. I turned around and pushed my way through the line of naked bodies. I squeezed through desperately, with my skinny body weaving through the people, and somehow made it to the back of the line. The dogs did not attack me when they noticed the movement because they were already used to my scent, and a dog would never bite the hand that fed him. It was getting dark, so there were fewer SS guards around. I am certain that even if an SS guard had caught me, he would have recognized me and let me go. My first move was to get out of that unforgettable Dungeon of Hell. Luckily, no guard had spotted me sneaking through the gate because they were all too busy handling the poor condemned Jews. That is how I escaped Sobibor.

By the time I exited the camp, it was pitch dark. All I could think to do was run, run, run. I did not know or care in which direction I was running, just as long as I ran far away from that horrific place and as quickly as possible. As far as I can remember, I ran all night until early morning. I must have covered some twenty- five miles that night. I ran through the deepest forest and underbrush to ensure no one would spot me. By this time, the Germans had put a price on the head of each Jew delivered to them. Each Polish civilian would receive a reward of five kilograms of sugar for every live Jew; the reward doubled if he were to kill the Jew himself. Every day, civilians would catch Jews and turn them in, so I had to be careful not to be seen by both Germans and Polish civilians. There was no option but to continue to run.

When I finally stopped running, I found myself at the forest's edge, completely exhausted, stark naked, half frozen and hungry like a wolf, but ecstatic that I was alive. The first thing I had to do was look for some clothes to cover my naked body.

From a distance, I noticed a scarecrow in a garden bordering the forest. I rushed to it and removed its clothing. Those rags were the first clothes on my body in almost thirty-six hours. I picked some vegetables from this garden and noticed a pile of hay into which I crawled and rested. I must have slept in this haystack for twenty-four hours. Once I awoke, I tried to orient myself to find my way back to my family. I walked for another two days until I reached my hometown.

Before I entered the Ghetto, I carefully asked questions to the right people. I inquired if everything was still the same and if it was all right for me to go home without endangering my family. I was told that nothing had changed. When I arrived at my parents' house, as before, everyone was glad to see me alive. Before this moment, they were all certain I had been killed. My parents updated me on what had been going on, all the raids by the Gestapo. It was amazing that they had lived through it while so many people in the Ghetto were killed during my absence. Half of the population of the Ghetto was gone, either killed or taken away to concentration camps. Like before, I resumed working alongside my father, doing the same work as before, for roughly three months. Then, my father received notice to work in another city about fifty miles away from our hometown, a city by the name of Chelm. Chelm had the largest jail in the area, also serving as an extermination place for all kinds of people. Once again, I would not allow my father to go, so I went in his place.

CHAPTER 3:

Working Day and Night

When I arrived in Chelm, together with many other Jews, the Jewish representative of the city was expecting us, along with approximately one hundred Gestapo soldiers. We were counted and separated into small groups and sent to various Jewish homes to room there. Every day, we had to walk ten miles to work, and after a hard day of slave labor, we had to walk ten miles back to our lodgings. I was placed with a small family, Mr. & Mrs. Friedman, and their daughter Sara, who was about my age. The first time I looked at Sara, I thought I saw Cinderella standing before me. She had a soft, round face, striking green eyes, and long, dark brown hair. She had the loveliest smile I had ever seen. I had never felt this way before. I found myself unable to look away from her face, which radiated like the sun.

As Sara whispered to me with her perfect lips that I should feel comfortable at their house, her voice sent chills throughout my entire body. She asked me to have a seat, so I did. Her mother and father then told me that the two of them were assigned work by the Gestapo, and the only person allowed to stay home was Sara. Sara took care of all the household chores and would now also take care of me. I was thrilled. Sara then asked me if I wanted anything to eat. Since it was Sunday afternoon, she asked me if I would like to accompany her on her usual walks down the street. We left the house together and began our walk while she explained the neighborhood to me. When we reached the end of the street, one could see the vast fields that resembled a large green cloud with the

14

sun setting behind it. Sara told me to walk down a little further with her to where she went every Sunday to watch the sun set.

We arrived at this magical place surrounding us with breathtaking flowers similar to tulips. I could not help but pick a large bundle of flowers for Sara. My actions touched Sara. We sat down, and she asked me all kinds of questions, such as where I came from, did I have any family, how many siblings I had, and if I knew who they were with and what they were doing. Finally, she asked me if I had a girlfriend or if I had ever had a girlfriend.

When I told her I did not, she laughed, put her arm around me, and gently kissed my cheek. This was the first time a girl had ever kissed me. It started to get cold, so I put my arms around her and kissed her. All I saw were stars. It was a moment I will never forget. It was getting late, so we headed back home. After dinner, everyone went to bed because the following day would be hard for us all. The next morning, Sara had a packed lunch ready for me as I left for my first day of work in Chelm.

About two hundred people from a dozen towns gathered at the place of work. First, we were all lined up, and the Gestapo officer looked us over one by one. He clarified that we Dirty Jews must remember we would have to work there and work hard. If we chose not to work hard, we would be shot on the spot. Immediately after his little speech, about thirty SS guards holding whips came out of a house and beat us. The first lash went over my shoulder. This was my first day of work in Chelm. I was given a wheel barrel, which could hold about two hundred pounds.

Pushing this load, I was expected to cover a distance of about one mile in five minutes. With each trip or fall, I would receive about a dozen lashes. This went on all day. By the end of the day, my body was almost cut into pieces. That same day, ten people were shot because they could not run fast enough with the full-wheel barrel. When lunchtime came, everyone had to stop where they were to rest and eat. Food was not provided, so we could only eat if we brought our lunch. When I stopped and looked around,

I saw Sara waiting for me with warm tea, which she had brought enough to give to a few people. We ate our lunch and continued to talk for half an hour. Once lunch was over, the noise of the whips started again. The SS guards changed every two hours, giving them the energy to crack their whips continuously. By the end of the week, half the people that had arrived at work were dead.

Sara had already planned how to spend the day together for my first Sunday off. First, she made us a delicious breakfast and then prepared a lunch bag to take to the same spot we had visited the week before. We talked and talked all day, and I can sincerely say that was one of the nicest days of my life.

The sky was a clear blue; not a single cloud could be seen, and the air was the cleanest I had ever felt. There was Sara with the soft touch of her lips. She kissed me again for the second time this week, but it was different this time. I started to cry because I was overwhelmed with emotions. I knew I was falling in love with her. We spent the day talking and kissing. When the sun went down, we headed back to her house. Sara's parents were waiting for us just as they had the week before, and Sara served us all dinner. When we finished dinner, Sara's father took me outside to talk. He started asking me questions like where we had been going and what we had been doing together. I was terrified. I was as scared of him at that moment as I was of the Germans. When he noticed I was petrified, he changed his tone and started talking to me as though he were my father, which comforted me. He asked me to marry Sara because he was unsure how long he would stay alive, and his dream was to see Sara get married. I was so surprised I did not know how to respond. After thinking briefly, I told him I loved Sara very much and would be honored to marry her. We all went to bed, and Sara made sure not to forget to give me a good night's kiss on the cheek. That is how my first Sunday off came to an end.

The next morning at work, the same routine started. We had to line up to be counted and assigned to various types of work. One SS guard called me out of the line this morning and ordered me to accompany him. I had no idea where he was taking me. Because I had no choice, I just followed him. His first words were, "Run, you dirty Jew," and then he started hitting me with the whip across my back. My mind raced with thoughts of what he would do the minute I started running. I was convinced this was some game for him, and I was going die that day. I ran for about a mile while the guard chased me with his whip until we reached our destination. It was the carpenter's shop where this SS guard was the master. One group was already working, and the others lined up for instruction. I joined the group, waiting for instructions. The SS guard told me to join those loading lumber, very heavy lumber, the kind used to build bridges. That is how my day at work began.

Just as the week before, Sara waited for me at lunchtime with some good things to eat and a nice cold drink. After a meal like that, I felt stronger and worked harder. I noticed another SS guard had been watching me work. The next morning, when we lined up to be counted, that SS guard called me out of the line and ordered me to come with him, but there was no whip this time. He interrogated me, asking where I had come from, where my parents lived, and so on. We rode a truck for about three miles to another camp. We arrived at a work camp that looked like others I had been at, with high fences surrounding a large building in the center resembling a hall.

The only difference with this camp was that it was deserted. He explained to me that this hall was the place where they would burn the dead bodies. He said he had been watching how hard I worked the day before and how well I worked for a small boy, so he took me there to give me a break. He said that with this job, I would not have to work hard and only guard this place at night. I was allowed to return home, but I would have to come back for my shift from eight in the evening to eight in the morning. That was great for me because first, I would not have to work too hard, and second, much to my delight, I could spend the day with my love, Sara. He told me that I would have to guard the place closely, and if I saw anyone around, I would have to report it to him immediately because no one was supposed to know what was happening there. Anyone that would come to snoop would have to be shot instantly.

I returned to the enormous hall for my first night of work. There were a few dead bodies there, but not so many just yet, and there was not much to do except for sitting and trying to stay awake. It was extremely scary, but if I did not do the job I was assigned, I would surely end up being one of the bodies in the pile. I continued to work there for about two weeks. One night, when I came to work, there was a lot of commotion going on; loads and loads of bodies were brought in due to a big "clean up" in the surrounding prison camps. After the bodies were dumped in the hall, they were lit on fire. At about three o'clock AM, the fire died down a bit. As I was watching the fire, completely horrified by this cremation of Jewish bodies, and nauseated by the intense odor, I noticed a body move and sit up right in the middle of the burning pile. There are no words to properly describe how I felt at this moment, other than I wished I was dead also because I could no longer stand the sight.

For a moment, I was paralyzed with fear, and then, as I came to my senses, I started running like crazy. All I could think about was going home to my family. At first, I had no idea where I was running to; I just ran away from the fire as fast as possible. Once I calmed down a bit, I turned toward my hometown. As usual, I could not walk during the day, so I walked at night and rested in hiding places along the way during the day. I ate anything, such as grass, herbs, and weeds. It took me about two weeks to reach Wlodawa. Just as before, I took all the same precautions before entering the town.

As expected, my family was thrilled to see me alive. Nothing had changed except for the fact that the Ghetto was less populated because many had died of sickness, had been executed, or were taken away to concentration camps. My father was still doing the same job, so I joined him at work. I was pleased that my friends were still working for him. Everything seemed

18

to be the same; however, now there were Gestapo raids every morning, leaving fewer people in the town.

One morning, we all had to report to the Marketplace for inspection. This time, we hid my mother, sister, brother, and grandparents in a tunnel my father and I had built at night under the ground floor of our house. This tunnel was where we would hide to avoid the morning raids. Only my father and I went to this general inspection where everyone was loaded on a train, except for the Jewish Ghetto police and other Jewish officials. Our destination was the crematorium at Sobibor, where I had worked before. About five thousand of us marched to the train station located about three miles outside the town. We were treated like cattle. When we realized our destination, men, women, and children started to cry and lament, praying for God to hear us in our plight. By the time we reached the train station, about one thousand people had been shot or had been trampled to death by others. I estimated that about one hundred Germans were watching us, so I pleaded with my father and friends to make a run for it to save our lives or to attack the Germans, being that we were now about four thousand people and could overpower them.

If we made a run for it, they could not kill all of us, but we could kill them and save at least half of our people. Everyone said no, that we could not do such a thing, and continued to believe that God would save us.

With this hope that God would save us at the last moment, we all were driven like cattle to the boxcars of the waiting train. By six o'clock in the evening, the train rolled. German guards were posted on every car, one on the top and one on the end. The windows were covered in barbed wire. My father was a sheet metal specialist and was carrying his tools, which included wire cutters. I grabbed the cutters from my father's tool belt and cut the barbed wire into pieces. I told him I was leaving this train and pleaded with him to come with me.

Because I was a small boy, I could not reach the window by myself and asked my father for help. My father blessed me and then helped me up to the window. First, I put my legs through, and then my body. When I was completely clear of the window, only holding onto the window frame, I let myself fall in the direction the train was going. When I hit the ground, the Germans opened fire, but because I was rolling down the embankment, they did not get me. Once again, I was safe from death, for now.

As soon as I stopped rolling, I began running in the same direction as the train. After about one mile, I saw my father, Jack, and Joe jump out the window. I was so happy they decided to take the chance and fight for their lives and that we were united once again. As usual, the only protection at this point was to hide deep in the forest with the help of my father, who knew the area very well. We started heading back to town, where my family was hiding in the bunker beneath our house. We walked all night until the next morning. We decided to stay hidden until nightfall to avoid being noticed when entering the town. We came across an abandoned barn where everyone fell asleep, closely packed like sheep.

Once it got dark, we moved out of the barn, one by one. We headed toward our house, knowing our family should be safe since no one knew about the bunker. Carefully, we snuck through the streets, around the corners, jumped fences, and arrived at our house. My father went to a specific spot where he sent out a pre-arranged signal to my mother, letting her know we were outside. We opened the hidden door, and all four of us entered the bunker. The room was about five feet high and wide and eight feet long.

CHAPTER 4:

Underground

Eleven of us were in that bunker hunched close together, facing one another. There was no food or water, and it was terribly hot. Breathing grew difficult because there was not enough air for all of us. After the third day of being cramped in this bunker, we awaited nightfall before venturing out to search for food and drink from other homes to bring back to the others. There was no running water in the houses, so the only drink we could find was stale water people had left behind or rainwater. We lived like this for about one month until the German SS and the Gestapo declared the area Judenrein, which means clean of Jews. Before they could declare Judenrein, they did thorough searches of each house one by one. Due to the ongoing raids, leaving the bunker at night for food became too dangerous. We were left with no other choice but to stay in the bunker for one week without food or water. I could not take it anymore. I started to cry to my mother and told her that I was dying of thirst. My mother desperately wanted to help me, so the only thing she could think of was to put some of her urine on a handkerchief to wet my dry and cracked lips. The taste of urine is something no one should ever have to experience. It was as though someone had lit my mouth on fire. I reached my limit and was ready to risk my life for a glass of water. I told my father that I was leaving the bunker. He refused to let me go. I pleaded with him to let me and my friends search for water and a better hiding place where we could still be safe. He would not listen to me; he wanted to wait a little longer, just a few more days. I was sure that the Germans were coming closer to our bunker as each day passed. I was also sure that they would eventually find us because of the evaporation that looked like smoke coming out of the air holes of the bunker that would surely give us away. Police dogs that were solely trained to find Jews always accompanied the SS guards. I continued to beg my father, but he would not give in, so I decided not to wait any longer and left the bunker. Joe, Jack, my cousin, and my sister Pesa followed me. We ran and ran until we reached the forest that would provide cover for us.

By now, it was the beginning of May. We walked about ten miles deep into the forest and set up camp. We stayed there for about a month. We drank when it rained, and all we could find to eat was some unripened fruit. After eating those green berries, our bellies started to swell, which made it hard and uncomfortable for us to walk, so I decided to go alone. I crawled on all fours the entire day until I reached the edge of the forest. The first thing I found was a small running stream. I threw myself into the water to cool and clean my sore arms and legs.

After being in the water for some time, I regained my strength and could finally get up on my feet again. I continued to walk until I spotted a farmer working in his fields. With careful planning, I located his lunch box, snatched it without being caught, and immediately returned to the camp where the others desperately awaited me. Once I arrived at the camp, the minute they saw I was holding something, they all attacked me like wild animals. I was forced to knock two of them down to regain control so that I could divide the contents of the lunch box into equal portions for all of us. We devoured the food. After we ate, they all begged me to find a safe hiding place until the war ended. How was I supposed to know where to find a place like that? I was the younger of my two friends but still looked at as the leader. All I knew was that I would do anything to survive. To survive, we had to have weapons, and to obtain weapons, we would have to kill.

I decided to visit an old friend of my father's who lived on a farm in the middle of a large forest about twenty miles away from our present hideout.

I had to figure out how we could all get there safely. It was too risky for all of us to walk together during the daytime, so we decided to wait another day to figure it all out. That night, one of my friends and I went to a nearby village, broke into a farmer's barn, and stole enough food to last about one week if it was appropriately rationed. I left Jack in charge and headed out to my father's friend alone. It took me two days and nights to get there. When I arrived, he was happy that I was alive. I told him the whole story. He brought me to a place near his house, where he had already prepared a hiding place for himself and told me to bring my family so that he could take care of us with enough food to survive the war. He then gave me a horse and a large sack of food to take to my friends.

He told me I could release the horse when I arrived at the camp because he could find his way back on his own. It took me all day to return to my friends with all the goodies. Everyone was waiting anxiously for my return. They were all overwhelmed with joy when they saw me. My dear little friends did not know what to eat first. That was the first night we slept soundly until about nine the next morning. Unfortunately, it was too good to be true.

We had quite the awakening. Germans attacked us along with Ukrainian police, who had joined the Germans in their fight against the Jews. As I found out later on, the day before, while I was gone, some of our boys had gone out into the open, and someone must have spotted them and denounced them to the Germans. I woke up to the sound of the Germans shooting, and their police dogs barking. At first glance I could see there were many Germans and police officers. It looked to me as though there were more of them than trees in the forest. As usual, all I could think of was to run, run, run. I jumped up, grabbed Pesa, and ran away from the line of soldiers. We ran all day until darkness set in and reached the forest's edge, where we sat down to rest as we were utterly exhausted. I was convinced that the other boys had been killed in the skirmish because I had seen no one else run after I grabbed my Pesa. I tried to orient myself because I had no idea where I was.

We were hungry and thirsty because we had nothing with us and had left behind all the food I had brought back to the camp earlier. Eventually, it started to get cold. My sister could not stop crying; she was just a young girl. I held her in my arms and tried to warm her a little, but even when she felt warmer, she continued to cry because she was thirsty and hungry. While I tried to calm her down, I heard footsteps. I paid close attention to the sounds and heard someone taking a few steps, then stopping for a while, and again a few steps and stopping for a while. The steps were coming closer and closer. Because I was hiding inside the woods, and they were walking outside, I could see them, but they could not see me. When they were about to pass where Pesa and I were sitting, I heard them talking in Yiddish to one another, and then I instantly recognized them. It was my cousin and my friend Jack. I called them by their names because if I had called them any other way, those poor boys might have dropped dead from fright. They saw me and ran toward us. We embraced each other with cries of joy and kissed about a thousand times. I asked them what had happened, and they told me that Pesa and I were the first to escape. When they finally got on their feet, it was too late to follow our directions, so they turned the other way. They had to cross a firing line where the Germans were set up like a hunting party, and that's when Joe was shot in the leg, but they picked him up and dragged him along until they could not hear any more shooting. By then, it was already getting dark, and they left Joe in the care of another friend. The two of them went in the direction we had taken because they knew that would be the only way to find the both of us.

That night, we all were tired and tried to rest and regain our strength. By nightfall the next day, we set out to where Joe and the other boys hid. We found them after about two hours. They both seemed to have lost all their strength because Joe had lost a lot of blood, and they were both hungry. Pesa, who had always been handy helping my mother at home, made bandages from our shirts and dressed Joe's leg. All I could think of was that we urgently needed food, water, and a horse with a wagon. We started to walk, and in the first village we came to, we were lucky enough to come across a farmer who gave us some bread, a horse, and a wagon. I put a lot of hay on the wagon, enough to hide the boys under it, while Pesa and I sat in the front. We headed to my father's friend in the forest.

When we came to his property, I did not stop at his house; I continued directly to the barn he had shown me before, not to arouse any suspicion. Once my father's friend saw us, he was relieved we went straight to the barn because the Germans had been at the house an hour before looking for Jews. I told him we came to him because we had nowhere else to go. First, he gave us something to eat, and then we cared for Joe, who fell asleep immediately. He told me that we should stay a few days at his place until the raids by the Germans would be over, and then I should go with one boy to Wlodawa to bring the rest of my family. We walked mostly at night. The only time we would walk during daylight was if the woods protected us.

It took us three days to get there. We were even more careful than before. There was no one in the town anymore. It was like a ghost town. It was dark when we reached our house. All we could hear were the footsteps of the SS guard patrolling the town. When we entered our backyard, I almost dropped dead from shock. Everywhere we stepped, there were dead bodies. We tried to identify the dead; some were good friends, and some were strangers. And then came the moment that changed my life forever, a moment I will never forget. To my complete and utter horror, I came across the bodies of my father, mother, brother and grandparents. It was just too terrible. Jack fainted, and I wanted to pass out, also, but I could not let that happen. It took every bit of willpower to overcome the need to give up because I knew the others depended on me. I had to get back to Pesa and my friends. I knew I still had to be their leader because they would not know what to do without me. I miraculously maintained my composure, obviously still in a state of shock, and once Jack came to, I immediately tried to calm him down. All I could do was pick out my family from the dead and try to give them a proper burial.

As I was moving their bodies, I heard several SS guards walking toward our backyard. I grabbed Jack, and we ran into our bunker before they came closer. I heard one of the Germans tell the other to stand watch until he was released. By noon the next day, the guards had been changed five times. We then heard wagons approach. These wagons were driven by civilians coming to load up the bodies. From their conversation, I understood they were going to take the bodies to a Jewish Cemetery. This was of great relief to me because I would not have been able to go on, not knowing that my family would have a proper burial. Years later, I found out that they did not give them a normal burial; they just dumped all of the bodies into one mass grave, and to this day, I still do not know where that grave is. We waited in the bunker until dark and then headed back to the farm. While in the bunker, we picked up all kinds of clothes my family left behind. We had a hard time carrying such a big load but had no choice. Everyone needed clothes. I also wanted to give some of the clothes to the farmer to show him our gratitude for his kindness.

It took us several days to return to the farm as the heavy load slowed our pace. Back at the camp, everyone was worried about us and were sure something had happened. They thought that if we didn't return, the farmer would turn them into the German authorities so that he could be rewarded with ten kilograms of sugar. By now, Joe was feeling a lot better. I gave the farmer all the clothes we did not need, and he was extremely grateful.

The time had come to tell everyone what had happened back home. They were all devastated. My family, particularly my parents, were deeply cherished. All my friends and cousins felt as though my parents were their own because they always made an effort to help everyone. Their passing deeply affected all of us. We wept and mourned for seven days. Then it was time to think about what to do next to survive.

CHAPTER 5:

Fight or Flight

It had become clear that we could not stay much longer on the farm because the farmer would also run out of food for his family. I let Pesa stay on the farm with Joe until his leg healed completely, and the rest of us would go out and see what we could find. The farmer agreed, so we left. Where to, we did not know.

I remembered that I had heard from another farmer that there was an area where they were organizing a Jewish Partisan group. We spent four weeks searching this area that was in the middle of the woods in the swamps. We walked the woods day and night, trying to find the group. Now and then, we emerged from the woods to beg for some food at a nearby farm or village before returning. Winter set in, and snow fell. One moonlit night, I found some footsteps in the snow. We followed these footsteps that eventually led us deep into the woods. Suddenly, I heard someone yell, "Halt! Do not move!" One shot from his rifle brought about one hundred men running. All these men were heavily armed with rifles, machine guns, and all kinds of antique weapons. As they approached, one man exclaimed, "Hey, boys, it's Bolek from Wlodawa!" Bolek was the name everyone from my hometown knew me by. They all gathered around and were glad to see us. My friends threw us a grand welcome party at their organized camp that lasted until the following morning.

That morning, the Commander called me to his tent. He explained to me that we would be able to stay with them only if I obtained my own rifle.

He gave me three days to return with a rifle or pistol; otherwise, we could not stay with them and be part of the group. I was disappointed and confused because I had no clue how to get my hands on a rifle or pistol. I took a long walk around the camp so that I could be alone and come up with a plan. It was a cold evening, and I started thinking about my parents, brother, grandparents, and first love, Sara. I needed her so badly at that moment. I yearned to talk to her like the way we would talk for hours on Sundays at our meeting place but now there was no one. The only person I had to depend on was myself. I had to forget about Sara and start focusing on my mission. It was late, so I returned to the camp. As soon as I got back, the Commander called me in again, but he had good news this time. I thought he had changed his mind about the task, but I was mistaken; he had another plan. He told me that a gentile boy had just arrived and wanted to join the group, and he, too, had no weapons, so the two of us had to go together to look for one. He called in the other boy and introduced us, "Bolek, this is Adasz." I shook the boy's hand. The commander then ordered us to leave and only return when each of us had obtained a rifle.

Adasz and I walked out of the Commander's tent and sat down for a long talk. He told me that he came from a nearby village where at least five to six German soldiers were patrolling the area. As I spoke German, I asked Adasz to explain exactly where this post with the German patrol was located. The next morning, we were on our way to his village. It took us about five hours to get there. We sat down, looked everything over, and worked out a plan.

Spring was nearing and the snow had partially melted, revealing patches of grass in some areas. It was quite a beautiful, warm, and sunny day. When we walked closer to the house where the Germans were posted, I noticed three of them cutting wood for the oven, and the rest were asleep inside. We approached the working Germans and said, "Good morning." We told them we would be willing to do their work for them in exchange for some food. They agreed and gave us something to eat first.

28

The Germans said they were going to take a nap and asked us to alert them if we heard any other Germans approaching. We agreed to their request. Then, they stacked their rifles into a pyramid formation and went to sleep. After a while, I told Adasz we should grab a rifle on my command and run without looking back. I went ahead and gave the order. We both sprung toward the pyramid, got hold of a rifle, and started to run like hell. There was only one problem: we both grabbed onto the same rifle. I was holding the top, and he was holding the bottom. We started fighting for the rifle as we ran, as neither wanted to let go. The noise awoke the Germans, who immediately shot at us. Adasz was hit in the leg. I picked him up over my shoulders while he still would not let go of the rifle and kept running until I reached the forest.

Luckily, the Germans gave up pursuit once we were out of their sight. I rested and bandaged Adasz's leg, which was bleeding profusely. We began to fight again over the rifle. We agreed to both hold on to the rifle until we reached camp.

I cannot remember how we made it back with Adasz on my shoulders and us both refusing to let go of the rifle, but we made it back. Once we arrived at camp, Adasz fell off my shoulders as we both rolled on the ground, fighting wildly for possession of the rifle. Everyone gathered around us, watching and not knowing what to do until our Commander appeared and took the rifle away. The doctor took care of Adasz's leg. I had no idea what was going to happen but was quite confident that the Commander would give the rifle to me. The next morning, everyone was waiting for the Commander's decision. He came out of his tent with the rifle, looked around, and said, "I believe this rifle belongs to Adasz. Is anybody against this decision?" No one said a word, and the rifle was handed to Adasz. I was devastated but knew I had to abide by his choice. The Commander then said to me, "Don't worry, Bolek. I have a new plan for you to make you a hero!"

The next day, the Commander and I took a long walk, during which he explained the following. About twenty-five miles from our camp, there was a central road no longer being used except for German military purposes. On this road was an old wooden bridge where German patrol cars would pass slowly, approximately three times a day. He told me that I should go to this bridge and take the Germans there as prisoners. When I heard this, I became so scared that the hairs on my head practically stood up. I could not believe I would have to do such a thing. I was just a fifteen-year-old boy who wanted to be in school or play with friends. The Commander left me no choice. If I came back without a rifle, I better not come back because they would have no use for me.

At around five o'clock the next morning, I started on my mission. I walked all day and night until I reached the central road. I laid down and slept for a while, enough to get a good rest. When I woke up I noticed that daylight was breaking so I moved close to the road, looking for that wooden bridge.

It took me about an hour to find it. I tried to figure out a plan for the ambush, but nothing came to mind. When I started this operation, I wondered how to stop a German patrol car alone, especially without any weapons. I then remembered something I used when I visited farmers for food. I would have to have protection for those trips, so I made myself a rifle out of wood. Well, something that looked like a rifle.

When you looked at it from a distance, it appeared as though you were looking into the barrel of a real rifle. For this operation, I took this fake rifle with me. I noticed a booth on the bridge that the Germans had previously used as a rain shelter, but there were no Germans around, and it was vacant. I entered the booth. I shoved the front end of my pretend rifle through the cut-out observation hole in the booth and waited. After six hours, I could not stand on my feet any longer, but I knew I could not leave my post because I was unsure when a German patrol car would come through. On both sides of the road were deep ditches. I wondered what I would do first when the German car would arrive. I knew the chances of a young, unarmed boy successfully ambushing a heavily armed German patrol car were close to none and that I would probably not make it out alive, but I had no choice. I convinced myself that the Germans had not gotten me yet and they would never get me like they did the rest of my family and all of my friends they had killed. I was going to fight to see them dead first before they got to see me dead!

As those thoughts circled my mind, I heard a car approach. The noise grew louder and louder until I could finally see the car. Three Germans were in it, one chauffeur, one Sergeant in the front, and one Officer in the back. Just before they reached the bridge, they slowed down to cross, just as my Commander told me they would. When they entered the bridge, the entire structure shook. They slowed down even more as they reached the middle of the bridge. I then started to scream louder than I had ever screamed, "Stop! Raise your hands above your heads, or I will shoot!" The Germans did as I told them to. I was extremely nervous. I had them right where I wanted them but was unsure what to do next. I ordered them to drop their arms and get out of the car. They obeyed.

I told them to come out of the car slowly, one by one, and walk away from the car about twenty feet into the ditch. Once they were lined up in the ditch, I jumped out of the booth, grabbed the biggest German machine gun, and started to run. That is where I made a grave mistake.

The machine gun was so heavy that I almost collapsed under its weight. When the Germans saw this and started making a move, I let off a few rounds to show them I meant business. I ordered them to undress and told one to tie up the other two. Once the two were tied up, I tied the third by myself. I was thrilled that I had made it this far. Nothing could stop me now. I then slipped into one of the German uniforms that fit me the best out of the three, but I still had to roll up the sleeves and tie them with a string so that they would not fall and get in my way. I had a hard time with the boots because they also were too big for me.

I then ordered two of them to sit in the back of the car, where I tied them securely once more and then had the chauffeur get into the driver's seat because he would have to take us back to the camp while I guarded him closely. I kept my gun aimed at him throughout the entire ride. After a few hours, we arrived back at the camp. When the guards around the camp saw a German car approaching, driven by a man in a German uniform, the alarm was sounded; everyone took their position and were all ready to pull their triggers. As we got closer, I stood in the front seat, waved my hands, and called out, "It's me, Bolek, the General!" Everyone was thrilled, and they all came to congratulate me on my successful mission. They all wanted to befriend me right away, but that was because they wanted to sneak into the car to grab some of the goodies I had in there. I kept a tight hold on the machine gun and warned everyone to keep their hands off the car!

I continued to the Commander's tent. There he was, like a different person, not like I knew him before. He immediately embraced me. He gave orders to get rid of the Germans. Some people recognized the Officer and Sergeant because they were guards in the Ghetto. The Commander looked in the car and picked out several things. I was not thrilled about that; however, I had enough arms to organize my own company. I asked the Commander if he had lost anything, and he dropped everything he was holding and said that he was just looking to see what a good catch I had made.

I told him he could have anything from the car except for the arms. I would keep the weapons for myself because no one wanted to come and help me with the ambush, so I deserved them all. We had a big party in my honor, where everyone celebrated my victory. After the party, the Commander announced that from now on, I would be an officer in his camp and that I should be treated as an officer. If anyone were to disobey my orders, he would be shot as a traitor. That night, everyone called me "The Little General." A nickname I proudly earned.

CHAPTER 6:

Love and Loss

The captured German car contained one heavy machine gun, half a dozen Tommy guns, one light machine gun, half a dozen rifles, half a dozen automatic guns, ten sniper rifles, and a lot of ammunition and hand grenades.

Jack and I returned to my father's friend's farm, where I had left Pesa and Joe. By then, we went like soldiers with two automatics, ammunition, and several hand grenades. At the first village we came across, we looked around and picked up some food, clothes, and other things we were sure the farmer would need. We loaded everything onto a wagon and continued to the farm. We arrived at the farm to find that everything was fine. Pesa, Joe, the farmer, and his family were all safe. After we took the food off the wagon, the farmer's wife prepared a wonderful dinner for us, so we sat down to eat and celebrate. At the dinner table, I told them how I became a General.

The farmer had two children, a daughter, and a son. His son was about thirteen, and his daughter Irka was my age. Irka gave me her special attention all evening, cared for me like a mother, and was extremely considerate. After dinner, everyone went to bed except for me. I was getting ready to walk around the house to see if everything was in order, being that no one else had done so. Irka showed up and asked if she could join me as I was about to go out. I told her that would be fine, and we walked out. Naturally, she was a big help to me, providing me all the information I needed, like the distance to the nearest Germans, and the location of the next neighbor and closest village. After going over my story again with Irka, she confided in me that she had been in love with me since the first time I showed up at the farm. At first, I did not believe her because I did not want to believe her. Irka looked like Marilyn Monroe, a beautiful girl with shiny blond hair and black eyes. She whispered over and over again, "I love you; I love you," until I could not resist any longer. I pulled her in my arms and held her close. Gently, I touched her soft lips with mine and wished that I would never have to stop. That was the night I fell in love again.

After three weeks, I had to go back to the Partisan camp. Pesa did not want to stay on the farm even though I wished she had because I knew she could have had a new life there. We all left, and I promised Irka I would be back soon, either to get her or send for her. The next day, back at the camp, I heard the news that within a day or two, the German SS soldiers would be getting closer to our camp with orders to attack and destroy us. I was ordered to command one company with about twenty people, including three friends and Pesa. That night, we broke down the camp and moved to another place about fifty miles away. It took us about two weeks to complete the setup due to the number of people we had, including women and some children. Along the way, we destroyed all German installations we came across, such as patrols, bases, bridges, and railroad tracks, and picked up all kinds of German supplies, including food. By the time we arrived at the new campsite, we had lost about twelve people and were all exhausted. At the new camp, we received a message that there was a concentration camp not too far from us holding about one hundred Jewish people and that the SS were about to execute them. I volunteered to help rescue them, but the Commander was against it. He told me that we should not get ahead of ourselves and that we must prioritize our protection first in order to survive.

I did not agree with him, and we almost got into a big fight. I told him I had a plan. I would try to rescue as many people as possible, but realistically, only half would be alive when I arrived. Out of the people I would rescue, I would pick out the strongest men, I would divide my firearms among them, and we would have the best Partisan group in the region. Combined with our fifty best fighting men, we would be able to form a regiment that would be able to take over the entire territory and give the Nazis a real fight. The Commander could not say no to my plan. I picked out ten men, including myself, and we headed out to the concentration camp, where we arrived at daybreak. As far as we were able to determine, the camp was guarded by approximately twelve SS soldiers. I devised a plan to attack immediately from the rear so that the front gate would be clear for the prisoners to use as an escape route.

We fought only on the outside of the barbed wire fence that surrounded the camp, and one of our men blew up the front gate with a grenade to give the people a way out. After about fifteen minutes, the fighting was over. The camp inmates ran so fast that we almost lost all of them. They disappeared in different directions. By dark, I had picked up about twenty-five boys who had not been able to run any further or faster because they were sick. I could not return to the camp empty-handed, so I took them with us. In about two weeks, the boys were in good shape again, and I taught them how to shoot a rifle. The truth was that I had never learned to shoot, but for some reason, it came naturally to me, and by the time I had them all trained, they were ready to fight. We were able to collect several more firearms from successfully ambushing German soldiers. At this point, half of my company was armed. This is how I created my first company of Partisan fighters.

By now, I was known throughout our region as the Little General. I received a message to come with everything I had to help the Jews escape the Ghetto of Warsaw and went directly to the Commander to discuss it. He did not want me to go and explained that we should not be fighting for others, but only for ourselves as a means of survival. I felt differently. I told everyone my plan and that they should get ready and stand by my side if they wanted to come with me. About fifteen boys joined me, including my three friends and Pesa. We did not waste any time preparing to leave. We paid a scout to guide us to Warsaw without any German interference. After about four weeks of marching, we ran into our first ambush. Eight of our boys were killed, including my little sister. I was devastated. To see Pesa shot right in front of me was something I will never forget. Hoping to rescue others, I had sacrificed my little sister. I could not believe that all of my family had now perished. That was the end of our rescue mission to Warsaw.

All I could do was turn back. It took us approximately five weeks to get back to our camp. When we arrived, we found the camp abandoned; everyone was gone. Immediately, I located our contact man, who always informed us about what was happening in the German world.

He gave me the bad news. About a week after we left, approximately ten thousand Germans and six German airplanes attacked the camp. Half of the occupants got away, and the rest were killed. We had no option but to camp on the same grounds because I was sure that the Germans would not come back as they had conducted a thorough search before they left. I told our contact to inform any of our men who survived the ambush of our whereabouts.

After a week of staying undercover, never venturing out into the open, all the boys who had survived returned, one by one. The last one to return was the Commander, accompanied by several Russians who had been active as Partisans, and one of them was an escapee from the German Police force. His name was Cola. He was about six feet tall and weighed approximately two hundred and twenty-five pounds. Then, there was Mishka, an officer of the Russian army, who had escaped from a German POW camp. There were two more men with them.

The next day, the Commander, Mishka the Russian, and I had a conference during which Mishka made an offer. He said he should be named our Commander because he was an officer and knew a lot about war tactics.

He said we should avoid the other Russians because he did not trust them. I did not have a problem with that, but our current Commander did not agree and did not want to give up his command. He said that Mishka the Russian was welcome to stay with us but that he would not be the Commander. Mishka accepted his offer and became one of us. That same night, Mishka warned me that we should keep a close eye because the other Russians planned to leave the camp and would cause trouble. Our Commander refused to believe this and ignored the forewarning. Just as Mishka had warned us that night, the other Russians left the camp unnoticed, taking with them several rifles, our only heavy machine gun, and the guard we always posted at the front of the camp. We found out later that they had killed the guard.

Our Commander was furious. He picked several of our best boys and set out to find the Russians to take back our weapons and avenge the death of our guard. It took them one week to catch up with the Russians in a village about twenty miles away. When our men arrived at the camp, they were unaware that the Russians had been warned of their approach and that they were expecting them.

When they entered the village, the Commander and our best men walked right into the Russians' trap and were shot one by one. We lost them all. It took us about two weeks to find out about their horrible fate.

We headed out to the village to collect the bodies so that we could give them a proper burial. After this incident, I clarified no outsiders would be allowed into our company. I decided we should all part ways and go underground for about two weeks, and then we would reunite. Everyone followed my instructions and left. It was wintertime, so it was cold, and the ground was covered with snow. I also could not stop thinking about my sister. All I wanted to do was return to my father's friend and my love, Irka, whom I missed terribly. After losing Pesa, the only other person I had left in my life was Irka.

I soon started on my way. It took me long to get there because it was winter, and I had to tread through the snow and ice. The Germans were continuously chasing us. It was almost impossible to survive because, by now, everyone was denouncing the Jews. When I finally arrived, everyone was thrilled to see me alive. They had heard from the other farmers about the ambush of our camp and were convinced that everyone had been killed. Irka, who I considered my girlfriend, was so happy to see me that she did not even give me a chance to talk with the others; she grabbed my hand and led me to a place where we could be alone. She took me to the barn. For a long time, we just held each other and kissed. Her kisses were so sweet that I forgot all my troubles. I had never met a woman as happy as Irka. It started to get late, so we made a bed in the barn in the sweet-smelling hay. I noticed her parents were watching us, so I did not want to disrespect or worry them. I walked outside and told them they should not worry, that we loved each other so much and would like to be by ourselves for just one night. I promised them that nothing improper would happen. The farmer told me that the one thing he loved so much about my father was that he was a man of honor who always kept his word, so he believed in me also, and he gave us his permission to stay in the barn all night.

We held each other close, and with a long, sweet kiss, we then fell asleep.

CHAPTER 7:

According to Plan

When we awoke the next morning, Irka's mother awaited us with breakfast. I can honestly say that this was the happiest time in my life. I know it sounds crazy for me to say this, but at the time, throughout all the pain that I had experienced, both physically and mentally, being with Irka made me happier than I had ever been before. I would still think about Sara and how nice she had been to me; however, with Sara, I never felt comfortable enough to tell her that I loved her. Saying I love you to Irka came naturally and straight from the heart. I was sure she was the girl for me. We were waiting for the war to end so that we could marry.

I stayed with Irka and her family for a few months until mid-summer. Everything was so beautiful and pleasant that I did not want to think about going away. I loved Irka more than anyone I had loved before. Even as I write this, I can still clearly remember that love. Irka and I planned to get married as soon as the war ended, and her father agreed to give us a piece of land to build a little house where we could spend the rest of our days together. Irka was Christian, but it did not matter to her whether we had a Christian wedding. Although her parents were religious, it did not matter to them how we would get married because they already felt as if I were their son.

One Sunday afternoon, while Irka and her family were in church, a friend from our Partisan company arrived with bad news. He told us that German soldiers had surrounded ten of our boys, and they were not far away. They had been hiding in the camp and had not had any food or water for more than a week because the Germans were waiting until they came out to surrender. I did not want to waste a minute, so I left to find some other boys to help rescue our men.

It took us two days to find twelve boys, and I devised a plan. We would attack the Germans at night and lure them away from their location while, in the meantime, one of us would establish contact with the encircled group and tell them of our intentions.

This is exactly what we did the following evening. Once we had drawn the Germans about two miles from the site, one of our men went to speak to the trapped group. We fought until the early morning hours and then disappeared into the forest. The Germans were puzzled and did not know what was going on. Our man had brought the other group food and water. We gave the men two days to regain strength, and then I proceeded according to plan. We attacked the Germans from the outside while the other group started shooting from the inside.

The Germans were surrounded and did not know what to do, so they went crazy, running like rats. All we had to do was sit on top of a tree and shoot at them one by one. Once it became dark, the situation was under control, and we reunited with the other boys. We were thankful that everything went smoothly. We waited a few days until everything was quiet, and all the German soldiers had disappeared. We then collected all the firearms the dead Germans had left behind and took off to a place about fifty miles away. We set up camp and stayed there for several weeks to ensure the Germans believed it was all over.

We started running out of food and became hungry. I planned how we could steal food from the Germans instead of taking food from the local farmers. I began outlining a strategy for how we could pull this off successfully.

Some of the boys did not like my ideas but had no say in the matter. I first gave the order that if anyone was caught taking food or anything else from farmers, they would be treated as traitors and punished. Word of this spread around the area, and all the farmers were willing to give me all the help and protection I needed for my company. This was an enormous benefit. By now, my group consisted of twenty-seven boys. One day, my old friend Adasz joined us and brought friends and firearms. Now we were thirty-two strong boys with heavy machine guns, a Russian type called Maxim, four light machine guns, six Tommy guns, a few rifles, and some snipers.

We started to prepare an attack on the German barracks in a nearby town that housed approximately one thousand Germans. I sent Adasz out to prepare four wagons with a lot of hay and told him to drive these wagons to the German barracks at four o'clock in the morning where we would already be waiting for him.

When Adasz arrived at the gate, he reported to the German guard that he was delivering his contingents. At this point of the war, every farmer had to turn over 75% of their produce to the Germans. When the German guard opened the gate to let what he thought were farmers and their wagons through, a few of the boys jumped the guard and killed him by stabbing him in the back. They pulled him out of the way and undressed him. Adasz slipped into his German uniform and stood guard at the gate. We loaded everything we could onto the wagons and ignited fires around the barracks.

I had divided my men into two groups, one to load the wagons and the other to cover them. This operation took one hour, and I ensured all telephone and radio communication equipment was destroyed first. Once the wagons were loaded and the fires were blazing, we hurried out of sight as fast as we could, split up, and took different directions to confuse the Germans. They were too busy battling the flames surrounding the barracks to notice us. We met the other farmers who had been waiting for us with two more wagons, gave them part of our loot, and then returned to our camp.

The mission was a tremendous success. None of my men got hurt, the farmers were happy, and we were ecstatic. They were so thankful to me that they made me feel like I was the most important man in their lives. I was honored. This made me want to protect them, fight for them even more, so that they would all have freedom one day. I then began working out more plans. Adasz had described all the important strategic locations in the area, such as bridges, railroads, and central stations. After the last mission, I gave the boys one week to rest, enough time for them to regain their strength and for me to devise further operational plans.

The following Sunday, we set out again. I had split our men into two groups, one under my command and the other under Adasz's command, always to be able to attack from two sides. We began by destroying smaller installations, such as bridges. Then we moved on to patrol stations and then railroad stations. The first railroad station I blew up was in our town. Two trains with about fifty carloads were waiting there, ready to pull out to the Russian front. A week later, we attacked a railroad station in Chelm, which was a much bigger station.

That time, it was not so easy. The Germans counter-attacked, and we had to pull back. This was the biggest fight we had run into, and I realized that I had made a huge mistake. I had predicted that there would be counter from the usual number of SS guards at Chelm but had not expected there to be about two thousand troops firing at us from all directions. I should have planned this attack more carefully, but everybody pressured me not to waste time. Everyone was convinced that if we succeeded with this attack, the tides would turn in our favor, and we would end the war. We tried to retreat, but the only way was to keep the boys together, fighting until we had pulled our way out of the trap. As always, we ran as fast as we could. Previously, we had lost two boys in the attacks, but most of the time, everything went smoothly up until now.

After some hard marching, I halted the group to take count. Ten were wounded, and twelve of us were fine, which meant that we lost eight of our boys at Chelm. This was a tragedy. I decided we must treat the wounded before we go any further. I sent a few boys to the nearest village to find a doctor. Three hours later, the boys came back with a doctor. Unfortunately, he was more of a witch doctor than a traditional one. The village people would not even have him treat their horses, but we had no choice. The boys also brought back some food for us.

I did not want to waste more time, so I prepared two wagons for the wounded the next morning and asked four boys to accompany them. I dispatched the wounded to where I knew they would be cared for. After they recuperated, I would be notified, and they would rejoin us. All I wanted to do now was see my dear Irka. I told the rest of the boys to go to one of our hideouts and stay there until they heard from me, which would be in about four weeks. I notified them where I could be reached in case something important arose. I then headed out to see the love of my life.

CHAPTER 8:

The Unimaginable

It took me almost four weeks to get to the farm this time. As before, everyone was happy to see me, and we celebrated my return with a big dinner. After dinner, when I finished my talks with Irka's family, like the last time, she took me outside. This time, Irka had complaints and conditions. She first insisted we get married without further delay and would not let me go away anymore. She said that if I left, she would come with me. That was not possible. It would be too risky for her and the rest of the company. Marriage was also out of the question at that time. She did not care where we would marry; however, her parents wanted us to marry in a church. That would have been completely impossible, given that everyone in the village knew who I was, and the church was always filled with Germans. I would have been caught instantly. We argued all night. By the next morning, she saw that, realistically, it would be impossible for me to grant her wishes, so she agreed to wait longer to get married. Now that we had passed that hurdle, I enjoyed my time with her and her family. Every day was happier than the day before. Even as I write this book, I still feel the enchantment of those days with Irka. I can hear her beautiful words, feel her soft skin, and taste her warm lips.

A month passed, and I worried about the boys because I had not heard from them. Being with Irka made me forget all my troubles, so I stayed with her for one more week. During that week, I received word that all the wounded boys had recovered, had reunited with the other boys, and were all waiting for my return. They did not know what to do without me and

44

ran out of food and clothes. Immediately, I dispatched a man with some food for them. I paid for the food with a large gold ring I had taken from a German soldier at one of our ambushes. Because I had taken care of the boys, I felt I could stay with Irka a little longer.

I used this time to prepare myself for my departure. I had obtained new boots and new clothes, and Irka had made me a wool sweater.

Irka and I continued to take long walks around the farm that would one day be ours to raise our future family. She always told me she wanted our children to be just like me. On the contrary, I wanted them to be just like her. These loving arguments would always end with kisses and great affection. I did not want these moments to end, but deep in my soul, I felt something was about to go wrong. I sensed Irka felt the same, but neither of us wanted to admit our fears.

Three days before my planned departure, the unimaginable happened. We had come home from our usual long walks, and Irka was making breakfast for her brother and me. I have not mentioned her brother Michael much because he had not spent a lot of time with us. He was a little boy with the mind of a little boy, and I did not have much in common with him. As Irka was cooking, I cleaned my gun. I took the gun apart, oiled each piece, and put it back together. I picked up the gun to look through the barrel to make sure I had done a good job and that it was clean.

Every time I cleaned my gun, I made sure I could see the light coming through the end of the barrel. As he saw me do this, Michael said, "Bolek, I am not afraid of you right now!" Then, bending halfway down, he added, "Just try to shoot me!" Irka joined in on the game and said, "Yes, Bolek, go ahead and shoot him, so he will be good to me next time you are away!" Since I was sure the gun was empty, I played along with him, aimed the gun at him, and pulled the trigger. To my complete and utter shock, a shot rang out of the gun, and Michael dropped to the floor. He was dead. I could not believe my eyes. What had I done? What happened next was something so devastating that even with all the torment I had endured up until that moment, I could not imagine it in my worst nightmares.

As I got up to run to Michael, I looked up at Irka, standing directly behind him, and noticed that she was holding onto the stove and slowly losing the strength to hold herself up. Suddenly, Irka collapsed. I did not understand what had happened. I pulled the trigger of an empty gun, and a shot came out, just one shot, and now Irka was also lying lifelessly on the floor in a pool of blood. I lost my mind, threw myself over her body, and fainted. When her parents heard the shot, they came running in and found all three of us on the ground. They thought we all were dead.

When they realized that only Michael and Irka were the ones who had bled and I was not shot, they tried to revive me. When I came to and looked at Irka's lifeless face, I collapsed again. This happened about a dozen times.

As devastated as her parents were, they knew this was a freak accident and somehow found it in their hearts not to hate me for taking their children away from them. The next day, we began to prepare for the funerals. Her parents did not allow me to attend because they were afraid that someone would denounce me to the Germans. I waited until night and then went to the cemetery to visit Irka's grave. This was the end of the greatest romance I have ever experienced in my entire life. When I returned home, her parents did not ask me to leave; on the contrary, they wanted me to stay with them. They wanted me to stay with them until the war ended, and then they would adopt me because they already saw me as their son. They knew that if Irka were alive, I would have become their son anyway and believed that should not change even though she had died. I would have liked that very much and knew that these people had done what my parents would have done for me, and I loved them deeply, but I could not do it. All the other boys' lives depended on me, and I could not abandon them. I promised them that after the war, I would return and live with them for the rest of my life.

I stayed one more night. Irka's mother knew that whenever I returned to the boys, Irka would prepare all kinds of goodies for me, such as food and clothes, and she always walked with me to the next village where her uncle lived. We would then say our goodbyes, and she would stay overnight at her uncle's, and he would take her home the following morning. Irka's mother wanted so much for me to feel as though Irka were still alive, so she prepared food and clothes for me and accompanied me on the way. All we did was talk about Irka. As I parted with Irka's parents, even though I promised them I would return, I knew deep in my heart that this would be the last time I would see them. Their last words were that I should not forget that they are now my parents and will always worry about me. We kissed each other goodbye, and her mother broke down and began to weep.

CHAPTER 9:

Back in Action

I was now on my way to meet the boys who were already expecting my arrival. This was because I had run into a few of them on my return journey, and one had gone ahead of me to notify the rest that I was en route. Due to the forewarning, there was a big reception waiting for me. Their Little General was back. The first action I took the next morning was to count all the boys and take an inventory of our arms. I counted twenty men equipped with arms and a lot of explosives. Everyone was well-rested and ready to fight. Even though we were ready, we had a big problem. The German army was moving back from the Russian front, and daily, it became increasingly difficult to operate in this area. It was time for us to move out. The only place we could go was the other half of Poland, which the Russians occupied in 1939 but the Germans captured back from them in 1941. This territory was on the other side of the river Bug and was well suited for us because of the dense forest and large swamps. We figured the Germans would not go there because it was nearly impossible to access for those unfamiliar with the forest. We also were told that large groups of other Guerilla fighters camped there. I grew up in that area, so it was very familiar to me, and I would not have a problem navigating it.

According to the plan I had worked out, we had to march about sixty miles until we reached the river Bug, where we would cross the river, hopefully without German interference. Since we could only travel at night, arriving at river Bug took about a week. The riverbank where we were standing was covered in low bushes; however, on the other side of the river, the horizon was lined with tall pine trees and appeared to be free of Germans. It was six o'clock in the morning, and due to the daylight, we could not all cross the river. We did, however, need to take advantage of the daylight to scout out the best place for us to cross since many of us could not swim. We had to make sure we knew where the water was shallowest. Two of our best swimmers volunteered and entered the river. Everything was going fine until two German patrolmen spotted them and started firing. Thankfully, they were too far away so they were not harmed and crossed the river safely.

Some knuckleheads among my boys returned fire on the German patrolmen without waiting for any orders. I knew that if we had remained quiet and not provoked the patrolmen, many of us could have safely passed once the Germans moved on. However, one of the patrolmen was killed, and the other escaped. This was the worst possible outcome for us. I had to think fast. We had no option but to cross the river at once because, without a doubt, the escaped German would bring back reinforcements, putting us in grave danger.

I told everyone we had to cross the river immediately. They all objected because many could not swim and did not think they could cross fast enough. As we all got into a heated argument about it, we did not notice that about twenty German soldiers were moving up the river, and several German trucks were coming to meet them on the other side. We still had time to make it, but no one wanted to follow my orders. They chose to wait for the Germans to pass, hoping they would remain unnoticed. This was impossible because the Germans knew we were there; they had police dogs that could smell us, and they would never have left without making sure they had killed each and every one of us. Finally, the Germans started closing in on us from both sides and let loose their dogs.

It did not take long for the dogs to find us. When the first dog attacked one of our boys, we had to fire at him, immediately giving our position away. I ordered two of our boys, who were armed with machine guns, to take position on either flank of our company and to hold off the Germans while some of us attempted to cross the river. This was not working because we presented too good of a target for the Germans, so I had to change my plan. I ordered the boys with the machine guns to cross first under our cover. This worked much better, and they both reached the other side. The two boys then opened fire on the Germans from across the river, making it impossible for the Germans to come closer to us. We all started to cross. We all made it to the other side, but unfortunately, five boys were injured. I immediately regrouped my men and marched them away from this place. All I wanted to do was get closer to the German/Russian front.

We marched all day without any food or water. It was a sunny day, so our clothes dried as we marched. Once it got dark, we set up camp to rest for the night. I sent a few guys to search for food. After a few hours, they returned with some bread, which we divided equally. Everyone was exhausted, so we all fell asleep, unfortunately including the two boys I had posted on night watch.

At daybreak, we were awakened by Russian guerrillas. We were surrounded by them, with their guns all pointed at us, just waiting for their Commander to give them the order. Then, a Russian officer arrived on a horse. He rode up to us, inspecting each of us one by one. He must have been approximately twenty-five years old, wearing a nice Russian Cossack-like uniform, with a Saber on his left side, a pistol similar to an American Colt 45, and a Russian automatic rifle, a PPSh, hung around his neck. Once he completed his inspection, he rode into the center of our group and called out for our Commander. I approached him and told him we did not have a Commander, but until now, I had been responsible for the group. He dismounted the horse and then asked if we were all Jews.

I demanded to know from him what difference that would make; regardless, we were on their side. He did not reply. In the meantime, another officer, also on a horse, appeared. This officer called out, "Hey, Mishka, come here." The Commander's name was Mishka. He walked over to the other officer, and they argued for a while. Mishka the Cossack then returned to me with several offers. The first was to give them all our arms and for us to return to where we came from. That was out of the question because the Germans would be waiting for us. The second was to join their group, but we would still have to give up our arms to them. I did not accept this either. He then told me that the only thing left for them to do was to take our weapons by force and have a shootout. He gave us thirty minutes to make up our minds as to which offer we would like to accept. I quickly realized we were stuck, and there was no way out.

I called the boys together and tried to think of a solution. To fight it out was out of the question because we were outnumbered twenty to one by the Russians.

Neither of us wanted to give up our guns, so the only thing to do was to join them under the condition that we would be able to keep our arms and that our group would remain together under their command. After thirty minutes, Mishka returned and yelled, "Hey, Moshka, come here!" I walked up to him with my automatic in my hands and told him, by his rank, that my name was not Moshka but the Little General. He laughed and said he had never seen a Jewish General before. I told him that I, the first Jewish General he had ever met, had killed more Germans than the number of hairs on his head. At that moment, I saw another Cossack approaching on a horse that seemed familiar, but I could not remember where I had seen him before. He approached us and began questioning our motives. He asked if we were Capitalists rather than freedom fighters, among other things. I told him that all I knew was that we had received orders from the underground in Poland, indicating that Polish General Wanda Waszilewska was in White Russia organizing a Polish Guerrilla army, and that we should try to unite with them. That was where we were headed, and if necessary, we would fight just as well as the Guerrillas of General Wanda Waszilewska. The other Russian officer was surprised and asked us to wait because he knew the location of General Wanda's camp. He mentioned that General Wanda did not like Jews, and then revealed that he himself was a Polish Jew.

I then realized where I knew him. I had met him in one of the German concentration camps near Hansk. At first, he seemed disappointed that I recognized him, but he got off his horse, shook my hand, and wanted to know how my name had changed from Bolek to the Little General. I told him the story, and he left for another conference with his officers. After several hours, he returned with food and water and brought us good news. The other officers permitted us to join them and remain a separate company under their command. We proceeded to march to their camp, which was located about ten miles away.

Their camp was in White Russia near the biggest city there, Pinsk. We had to cross a canal that connected the Russian river Pripet with the Polish river Bug. We entered the territory that belonged to the Guerillas, and the Germans stayed away because they were well aware of this. The worst part was that the Russian Officers did not stand by their word.

Upon our arrival at the camp, they ordered us to line up in a single file and sent us into a little tent one by one. Inside, a few Russian officers sat around a table, took our firearms, and then directed us to leave through the back entrance. Only after we had exited the tent did we realize that they had taken away all of our firearms. I made a big commotion, but no one wanted to speak with me. We felt helpless, as though our lives had been taken from us; without the firearms, we were lost.

We had to find some way to protest, so we staged a hunger strike and refused all food. On the third day, the Commander came to us. I had heard him being addressed as Tovarish Commissar. He walked straight up to me while I was lying on the ground and ordered me to get up. I told him I could not because I had not eaten in three days. He then yelled, "I will make you get up, you little contra-revolutionist!" He grabbed a rifle from another Russian and began to fire into the ground around me. Everyone shouted, "Get up! He will kill you," but I did not budge. At this point, I would not surrender to his order because I would rather be dead than be without arms. And that is what I told him. If he wanted me to get up, he would have to give all my boys their weapons back. Seeing my persistence, he agreed to return only my automatic. Then he asked me to come to his office, a small bunker in the middle of the camp. I walked straight into his office. He greeted me with "Tovarish Little General," the only name he knew me by, and asked me to sit on a half-broken wooden box. He then offered me a glass of Vodka. He was convinced that I would not be able to drink alcohol after having starved for three days and that I would make a fool of myself, providing him a good show. I took the drink as he sat down disappointed. I downed the glass of Vodka and asked him for a refill. All kinds of food were laid out on the table, so I binged. I cannot remember how much I ate, but I remember spending a long time eating and drinking with him. Finally, he stood up and told me I would have to stay with him because he liked my charisma. It was an order. Because of my diligence, he agreed to return all the weapons to my men, but they would have to be separated, assigned to different companies to serve with his people. I went out to my boys to discuss this with them and to see if they would agree to this. They all accepted the offer. I went back to the Commissar and agreed to the terms.

The following morning, I assembled my boys and gave them a choice as to which company they wanted to join. This was the first time we had been separated in all the years we had been fighting together, but we would still see each other daily. I was informed every time one of my boys was mistreated, and I would be right there making a commotion to make sure any Russian who was out of line would be punished. This happened all the time, which was extremely frustrating because I found myself fighting with the Russians on a daily basis. At least with the Germans, I could kill, but with the Russians, I could only use my fists. I didn't care, though; I always made sure to protect my boys.

CHAPTER 10.

Behind Enemy Lines

When my boys and I were separated, my Commander assigned me to the so-called Rosvitka Company. This was the most dangerous combat assignment, going behind enemy lines and taking important prisoners. He had told me he wanted to see if I was as good at fighting the Germans as I was with my mouth. Therefore, I was off to my first mission with three Cossacks. There were four of us, including one Officer. We were all on horseback carrying automatics, sabers, and pistols. Our assignment was to get behind the enemy lines and determine how many Germans were in this area. Once we obtained the information, we would destroy all German checkpoints, bridges, and important installations.

We rode all day and night until we reached the first German checkpoint. We picked up a local man who functioned as our scout on the way. He successfully led us around the checkpoints without being noticed. We continued to a little town called Drogichin, where we would begin our assignment. This town was the center for the delivery of grain that the Germans collected from the farmers in the area. Once the grain was collected, it would be sent to Germany. Within two hours, we had set the whole town on fire, including the grain depot. We did not leave until we were sure the town was destroyed.

We had to move fast to the next place before the Germans of Drogichin would have time to warn anyone. We mounted our horses and were on our way. I do not think we could have made it any faster with cars. After two hours, we reached the next German point. The Hungarians, who served with the Germans, were responsible for safeguarding this location, where the sole inhabitants were cattle. We destroyed the entire area, including all the livestock. It took us nearly three hours to complete the task, during which we had to do a lot of shooting because the Hungarians were putting up a big fight. There were approximately ninety Hungarians, and only four of us. We made it without much trouble because the Hungarians were not very good fighters. We continued to the next destination.

It was already dark by now, and we feared we might run into German ambushes, so to avoid populated areas, we went through the countryside. We were in dire need of rest. After several hours, we found refuge in a place belonging to the scout we had picked up along the way. Shortly after daybreak, we continued and sighted our next target, a railroad bridge. This bridge was heavily guarded, so our Officer decided not to attack as it would be too dangerous. I thought that if we returned to the camp without having completed one hundred percent of our mission, I would be the one blamed. I approached our Officer and told him that it would be quite easy to trap the Germans and that I already had a plan. All three laughed, called me "Moishe," and asked if I knew how to shoot around a corner. At that moment, I was at a loss for words, but since I always preferred to start the fight (the first fights were always the best), I picked up my automatic, placed my finger on the trigger, and pointed it at them.

They stopped laughing immediately and started shaking in their boots. I told them if they were so brave, they should go ahead and take a shot at me. The Officer apologized immediately and promised that this behavior would not repeat itself as long as he was in command and that if we made it back to the camp alive, he would give a full report to the Commander. I had to stay tough and make sure from then on that they would not pull any tricks and knock me off so that they would not have to explain anything to anyone, being that I was only a little Jewish boy. I proceeded to tell the Officer my plan.

I would take four horses, mount dummies on three of the horses, and take them through the town, firing like crazy in all directions while dropping hand grenades. That would cause all of the German soldiers in the area to chase after me. This would allow the Russians to cross over the bridge, come into town, and continue the destruction. He was speechless and extremely impressed. He took out his tobacco pouch and cigarette paper and offered me the chance to roll myself a cigarette. This was the first cigarette I had ever smoked in my life. It was a cigarette made from Russian Mahorka, an extremely strong tobacco. After the first drag, I almost passed out but could not show him that. I had to maintain my composure.

As we continued to smoke, he opened up to me and told me his life story. He told me that he was a good friend of the Jewish people, which I did not believe. I never trusted people who tried to win my confidence by saying their best friends were Jews. Especially because he laughed along with the others when they called me "Moishe." I told him exactly how I felt. He then took a picture out of his pocket and explained that it was his family. In the picture, there was a little girl, a young boy, and his wife. He confided in me that his wife was Jewish, and I had to promise him on my honor that I wouldn't tell anyone. I promised him that. At this point, my feelings toward him slightly changed, and I began to trust him a little more. He then called over the other Cossacks, explained the plan, ordered them to prepare the horses, and handed them over to me. Once the horses were in my care, the Officer told me to wait until they got closer to the bridge. Once they reached the bridge, I could start my rampage. I waited about twenty minutes until I was sure they had taken their positions, and then I started.

Just like I had planned, I rode into town, firing my gun as fast as I could, creating as much smoke and dust behind me as I could so that the Germans would be unclear how many of us there were. Exactly as I had expected, I had the entire German force of that area on my tail. All the Russian men had to do was get rid of one guard at the bridge. After I rode out of town,

I chased the other three horses in different directions, causing the Germans following me to split up. After approximately an hour of being chased by the Germans, I managed to lose them and circled back to town to meet the Russians, but only with one horse. When I got closer, all I could hear were explosions everywhere. I found my group, but they were quickly disappointed because the other horses were not with me. The Officer asked me where the other horses were, and I asked him how he could expect me to do all of this without losing a horse. I told him I knew this would happen but did not want to divulge it when I told him the plan because I knew he would not agree and the mission would never have been accomplished. He understood my position and was on my side because we succeeded in the mission. The others were still angry with me. If it were not for the fact that the Officer defended me, the others would have shot me right then and there.

We continued to move on and walked all day and night to meet another farmer who was an ally. We stayed overnight with him, and he provided us with fresh horses.

The farmer informed us that a large German army unit was retreating from the front lines not far away, and they were based exactly where we were planning to cross the river. We had no choice but to stay with him for the time being. The other Russians did not mind because all they cared about was drinking Vodka and eating. Under these conditions, they would not have minded spending the rest of the war locked up at the farmer's house. I, on the other hand, could not rest knowing there were so many Germans near us, and no one was doing anything about it. I asked the officer what he planned to do, and he answered that we had done enough already and were entitled to a few days of rest. I did not like his attitude. I felt that this was our opportunity to accomplish something worthwhile. I requested permission from the Officer to go with the scout and take a good look at the German movements. He allowed me to do so. We rode our horses close to the main road because it was a good observation point since we could easily see the Germans' every move. After a while, I noticed that one

German column with half a dozen wagons and horses was separated from the main train and left behind without escorts. I thought it would be good fishing for us. I sent the scout back to fetch the others. In the meantime, I followed the Germans to see if there were any changes. After an hour, the Russians returned, accompanied by the scout and the farmer. We talked the situation over. Everything seemed to be in our favor because the situation had not changed.

Since it was getting dark, I did not want to lose time and felt it would be best to attack immediately and take the wagons. Some of the others hesitated and thought it would be better to wait a little while longer. I argued that if we were to wait, we would miss our opportunity because it would be too dark, and we still needed some light to accomplish the mission. If we were to start immediately, it would be pitch dark by the time we completed the mission, and we could get away without any problems. The officer agreed with me, and we commenced the attack. Three of us started shooting from the front and the others from the rear. After we had fired a few shots, only one German returned fire, and we were able to shoot him down. The rest of the Germans did not fight back. Once again, another mission accomplished.

We returned to the farmer's house with the wagons and checked the contents. The wagons were loaded with food, clothing, and many other useful items, part of which we took with us, and the rest we left for the farmer. After resting for a few hours, we headed to our last target, a police station located directly on the canal. Here we were, the four of us with the four wagons we had captured, and we had no clue what to do. The one thing we did know was that we had to finish the mission. This time, they all came to me and asked me if I had any ideas. "Well," I said, "I know I am just a little Jewish boy, but I will tell you what I would do as a little Jewish boy." I explained to them that I would take the wagons over to the other side of the canal so that all we had to do was pick up the wagons and head back to camp when the job was completed. It would take us an entire day to bring the wagons to the other side because we had to cross the canal

58

far away from the police station to avoid being noticed. We would then return to the police station to finish the job. The only other option was for one of us to drive all the wagons to the other side of the canal while the rest of us attacked the police station. This was not a good option because there were about two hundred Germans at the police station and only four of us. We decided to take the wagons to the other side and return as a complete group. It took us longer, but it also gave us more time to make all the observations at the police station to ensure the success of our mission. It was to our advantage that the Germans were put up in three houses arranged in an open square about one block long and wide.

I used the same tactics as I always had, attacking in the early hours of the morning. It was a cold evening, and the Germans were sound asleep. They had guards posted every three meters along the canal. Many Germans were stationed there because it was a long canal. We found out that the guards changed every four hours, which gave us enough time between the changing of guards to accomplish our job. We waited in the bushes about two hundred feet away from the houses. First, we killed the guards standing around the houses.

Then, we placed dynamite at the entrance of every house and sprayed kerosene all around the buildings. We then separated since everyone had his job to do. One was to set off the dynamite; the other was in charge of igniting the kerosene. The Officer took a position on one side of the square formed by the houses, and I stood on the opposite side. Once the fire started, there would be only one way for the Germans to run, and both the Officer and I would be able to shoot them down one by one. We were prepared to change places should either of us fall out. The Officer and I started to fire at the houses, so the Germans came running out, but we made it impossible for them to go any further, so they turned back inside to take cover. The Germans returned fire from the inside and shot the Officer in the leg, but he continued to fire his automatic. With all the counterfire, it became difficult for us to keep shooting, so we ignited the kerosene. Flames shot up all around the houses, making it impossible for the Germans to continue to fire because the blaze blinded them. The next step was the dynamite, which completely blew up each house. We fought until we ran short of ammunition, and then I gave the signal to pull back. At that point, we noticed that one of the Russians had been killed, but the rest of us managed to get away safely. We did not stop anywhere; we just kept running until we crossed the canal.

Across the canal, a Russian Patrol was waiting for us because they had heard all the explosions and shootings and had come to help us. We were so happy to see them. They were surprised to see us because it had been more than a week, and they were convinced that we were all dead. The Officer told everyone that if it weren't for me, the little Jewish boy, they would have all been dead. When they heard that, all twenty men picked me up and yelled, "Hurray!" Once again, they considered me a hero, but I did not care to be one; the only thing that was important to me was showing them that a Jewish man is just like any other man. We retrieved our wagons from the hiding place where we had left them the day before and returned to our camp, which was still another twenty miles away. We rode on horseback with an escort of twenty men. I truly believed that if we could always have these men with us, we could win the war. Once we arrived at the camp, everyone welcomed us.

I had to shake hands with at least two hundred people. It was getting late, and we were exhausted, so we went straight to sleep.

CHAPTER 11:

New Orders

The following morning, the Commissar invited me to have breakfast with him. I accepted. Our breakfast included a table full of delicious food and plenty of Vodka for both of us. During breakfast, we discussed what happened on my mission, discussed our different points of view, and finally began to understand each other better. He told me that in two weeks, there would be another excursion of about twenty men to cross the front lines and enter Russian territory to meet the Russian army and help bring to them women, children, and all the sick. He expressed he would like me to volunteer for this mission. I accepted. With a few more glasses of Vodka and good wishes for the new mission, our breakfast ended. I learned how to live with the Russian people and to be more correct with the Communists. Initially, it wasn't easy because we did not speak Russian and did not fully trust one another, but now I was starting to understand more.

Ten days later, we all were assembled and ready to move out. We had one officer named Cola. Cola was a farmer's son from White Russia but was not a Communist; actually, his father had been sent to Siberia for being wealthy. Although he was not a Communist, he was still a Russian and a great defender of his Motherland. We had a heavy machine gun called a Maxim Tachanka. The Maxim is the gun's name, and Tachanka is the buggy on which the machine gun is mounted. It takes a crew of four to operate the Maxim Tachanka and three horses to pull it. Officer Cola came to me and told me that he had received special orders that I was to stay with him at all times and act as his assistant. This order came directly from the Commissar. We had an additional five wagons drawn by single horses and driven by local farmers. Each wagon carried food for us, the horses, the farmers, and five other people, including children. We pulled out at around six in the morning.

The first day was not so bad. The weather was mild, and the ground was dry, so we traveled a good distance. We split up our fighting troop into two groups: one riding in front, which included the Officer and myself, and the other that followed behind the wagons. After a long day's drive, we had our first night's rest in a little village somewhere in the swamps of White Russia. We drove all the wagons into a large barn and posted guards around the barn. Everyone else went to sleep.

It was still dark when we got up early the next morning. We assembled the caravan and moved out again on our way. The weather was once again on our side, so we were able to make good mileage. Unfortunately, it started to rain in the late afternoon, so we had to camp earlier than expected. We pulled into a small settlement that consisted of two houses, and as before, we picked one barn that would accommodate all of us. By daybreak, we were ready to move again, but the rain was extremely heavy this morning. We had to keep moving, or we would lose too much time. There were many Guerillas in the area, mostly Ukrainians, who called themselves by various names such as Bulbovcy, NSZ, Szekache, and Banderovcy, who were fighting for the Germans, so we could not stay in one place too long.

We drove on, but this time slowly, as it became harder and harder for the horses to pull the wagons. It was raining so hard that the wagons' axles were covered with water, causing them to sink deeper and deeper into the mud. We stopped at the first place we could find shelter for the women and children and where we could bathe the sick. It took us quite some time to find a place, and it was already dark by the time we did. Once we found a barn, we posted one guard, and because everyone was exhausted, we fell asleep immediately. During the night, the rain stopped, and then everything froze. We slept a little longer than usual that night, and it was already daylight when we awoke. Suddenly, we heard one gunshot followed by a stream of shooting. The barn walls were sprayed with bullets, causing them to look like a sieve on a water cooler. Even though our clothes had not dried overnight, we sprang up ready to fight but we were pinned down in the barn.

Finally, two other Russians and I managed to get out of the barn and take cover outside. One other man tried to get out but was shot the minute he stepped outside. The three of us who made it outside went in separate directions to provide better cover for the others as they tried to leave the barn. Our plan worked, and almost all our fighting men could get out, helping us set up a nice defense position. Fortunately, there were not that many attackers, and after a few hours, they retreated, leaving about ten dead people behind.

We packed up without any further delay and moved out. The weather had returned to be in our favor. Everything was frozen solid, making it easy for the horses to gallop, getting us far away from that place as quickly as possible. We could not waste a minute because the group that had attacked us would surely come after us with reinforcement. We were able to cover a great distance. By the time we reached the next stop, it was dark again. We had to stop at nighttime because of the possible ambushes, especially because we were now close to the fighting lines. It was much easier defending us in strange territory during the day than at night. We were defending not only ourselves but also the women, children, and the sick.

We estimated that we would have another two days of travel until we reached the back of the front lines. The only thing that concerned us was how we would cross the river Pripet. It was a wide river, with swamps about half a mile wide on both sides. Just as we had anticipated, it took us two days to reach the river, and once we settled down for the night, we worked on a plan for crossing the river. After thinking all night, I came up with a plan. I remembered that one time, back home, a lot of snow had fallen and several wagons had gotten stuck. The drivers of these wagons fabricated a type of sled, mounted the wagons on them, and moved them on their way. I suggested we do something similar and make rafts for the wagons to float on. We mounted all the wagons on timber and pulled them to the water's edge. We planned that the next day, a few men with horses would swim across the other side of the river with long ropes fastened to the wagons, which were all tied together. With the horses pulling the wagons from one side and us pushing them from behind, we would make it across in a few hours.

It took us the entire day to set up this operation and have everything ready for us to cross the river the next morning in the shortest time possible under the circumstances. Once again, I could not sleep the entire night. I was anxious to see all of us on the other side of the river.

The following morning, we began our operation just as planned. Everything was going smoothly until suddenly when we were about halfway through the river, two German fighter planes showed up and opened fire on our boys immediately. We returned fire but could not even nick them with our small arms. Several of our boys were killed instantly, and one of the wagons, the one with the children, had torn loose from the other three and was floating down the river. We all started to swim to this wagon, leaving the other three wagons unattended. After a long argument, I convinced everyone to let the wagon float away, as it would stop somewhere along the other side of the riverbank. The most important thing at this point was to get the other three wagons across quickly and safely and then look for the wagon with the children. The German planes returned and made another pass on us, spewing fire from all their weapons, but they left the wagon with the children alone. This was what I had anticipated. It took three more hours before we were all on the other side. Once we had crossed, we could take cover in the bushes, making it harder for the planes to spot us. We picked up our wounded and dead and assembled again. I sent out six men to find the children. As it was getting dark, they returned with the wagon and the children, all unharmed but a little wet and exhausted from what they had just gone through. We set up camp and made a small, covered fire in a type of tent so that we could dry our clothes and keep the children and the sick warm.

The next morning, we faced a problem once again. We had no idea how to get out of this swamp. There was neither a road nor a path leading away from the river. All we could see was swamp and more swamp. We loaded two wagons with the women and children, put the sick on the horses, and left the other two wagons behind. We walked on foot, leading the horses. We walked the entire day without seeing an end to the swamps and had to stop to camp for the night. Most of us thought we would never get out of there. I was convinced that I would never find a way out. We set up camp in the middle of nowhere, and all everybody wanted to do was get a good night's sleep. We continued our journey the next morning, setting out in the same direction as the previous day. We could not walk too fast because we were up to our necks in the swamp, but we finally reached drier ground. We rested a bit and then continued. We were determined to find a way out and find it that day.

CHAPTER 12:

On My Own

After we arrived at dry land, we heard the sounds of heavy artillery behind us, which caused us to believe we were on the other side of the front lines. It took us about an hour to get to the main road, where we had seen Russian troops moving from a distance. When the Russians reached us, they stopped us at once and asked for identification. All we had was a password, which was not much help. The Russian patrol took us to their headquarters in the next town. When we arrived, we were recognized immediately because apparently, they had been expecting us for over a week. They took the sick, women, and children away from us. They gave us twenty-four hours to rest, with an order that everything would be ready for us to move out again and head back to camp where we came from after this time was up.

The next day, we awoke at around five o'clock in the morning. We fetched our breakfast from the military kitchen. The Russian Officer assigned to us then took us about twenty miles away, where everything awaited us for our departure. There were three Russian wagons. None of us knew what was inside them. They gave us a map with directions on how to get back. On the map, they pointed out where we would most likely run into Germans, and again, we were on our way back to the camp. We rode until late that night and then stopped to sleep. The day went smoothly because a Russian detail accompanied us. After they left us alone, I was curious to know what we were carrying in the wagons. All I could find was arms and dynamite, but no food. This presented an enormous problem for us. There was nothing we could do at that moment. Our officer did not know how we would make it without food. For me, it was simple. I told him that instead of getting food on the way, which would consume more than half of our travel time, I would return to the Russians with a few other boys and get food from the Russian army. The officer agreed, so I set out to the Russians. After several hours of travel, I returned to our men with a wagon of food. I was unaware that Russian patrol had followed me, comprising Russian MPs, and I was arrested the minute I entered the camp.

They tried to take all of us, but I insisted that this was my doing and that the others had nothing to do with it. They left the others alone and took only me with the wagon of food. Before they took me away, I told my officer to wait for me only twenty-four hours and, if by then I did not return, to continue without me. The Russian patrol took me back to the same place I had gotten the wagon of food and locked me up right away. They kept me incarcerated the entire day without any food or water. At around six o'clock in the evening, they took me out for interrogation as a traitor for stealing government property. But here again, I was lucky. The head man in this investigation knew my commanding officer; they had been in military school together before the war. He asked me why I took the wagon of food without permission. I explained to him the trouble we had getting there and what kind of trouble we expected on the way back if we had to look for food throughout our travel. He released me immediately and made a new report that the wagon did not belong to the Russians. He wrote I had captured this wagon from the Germans, so it belonged to me. I waited until the next morning, and they escorted me back to the camp, where I thought the other men were still waiting for me. When I arrived, no one was there. The escort turned back, leaving me all alone with the wagon full of food.

I was not too worried because I had another map with me and knew the others could not be too far away. I was sure I would catch up with them in a day or two because they were probably moving slowly, expecting my arrival. With these thoughts in mind, I started on my way. I traveled all night and day, only stopping to feed the horses, trying to catch up to the others as quickly as possible. It was my second day of traveling, and there was still no trace of them. Whenever I saw a Russian Column pass, I asked them if they had seen a small group of Partisans. The first one I asked told me they had seen a group resembling the one I mentioned the day before. They advised me not to go any further because a large German army was grouping ahead, and the Germans were pushing back. I could not take a chance of going back or waiting. I had only one thing in mind, so I kept moving on. I traveled until late evening and stopped when I heard artillery fire.

At first, I thought the Germans had spotted me. I took cover immediately and waited until it was completely dark to keep moving.

After a while, everything quieted down. I was about to move out again when I saw another large Russian detail moving back. I stopped and tried to find out what was going on. The Russians had suffered heavy casualties, and they warned me not to go any further. After they told me where the Germans were and in which direction they were headed, I was sure I could keep going and try to avoid them. What I did not know was that some crazy German officer had led his entire army into the swamps, ordering them to shoot anything that moved so that no one would come close to them. This is where I made a mistake. I figured the Germans would never be able to return from the swamps. At first, I thought I would get close to them and wait until they moved again, all the while staying close behind. I decided to go with another plan.

I circled the territory where the Russians had trapped many Germans. My plan was to reach the river and stay there until I could find a way to cross the river. I ended up right in between the Russian and German front lines. I immediately took cover and thought feverishly of a way to get out. The best idea I could come up with was to load as much food as possible on one horse, pull it with my horse, and leave the wagon behind. I continued like this all night, running every now and then into a German group that

68

would send a hail of bullets after me. I never stopped. I ran and ran, believing that somehow, I would get through the lines and soon the river would be waiting for me. At about six o'clock in the morning, I finally saw the river and cautiously moved closer, but then all hell broke loose. The Germans opened fire on me. I was convinced the entire German army was after me. Everything was being fired at me: artillery, machine guns, mortars. I had only one thing in mind: run into the river with the horses and swim to the other side. This was the only way left for me to get out. Somehow, miraculously, I made it to the river. About halfway across the river, I lost the horse with the food, but I could not let this horse go. I went through too much trouble on account of this food. I would not give up that easily. I went after the horse, and the Germans took advantage of my exposed position. They fired at me with everything they had.

I finally got a hold of the horse with the food and started to swim to the other side without thinking of the Germans. I could not see anything due to all the splashing in the water from the firing, and only by instinct did I swim in the direction of the other shore. When I finally reached the bank, I ran to take cover.

After a while, everything quieted down. There was no more shooting. I took advantage that there was still daylight to keep moving in order to orient myself and figure out in which direction to continue. Once again, all I could see was swamp. I had to slush through with the horses until nighttime. I had to stop and camp for the night because the horses were exhausted and refused to go on. I was too scared, so I lay awake most of the night. All I could hear were traffic noises like trucks, tanks, and airplanes. The noises gave me an idea of which direction to take the next morning. The following day, I headed out in the direction of the noises. After about an hour or so, I saw a deserted road. I tied up the horses and moved out to investigate the situation. I approached a little house on the road. In the house was a little old woman. I asked her about the noises from the night before, and she told me they came from Russian army movements because several Russians had stopped at her house for food and water. I asked her if she had seen any Partisans, and she told me that two days prior, a group with two wagons, accompanied by a dozen men, had passed by. She pointed out which direction they had taken. I estimated I could catch up to them within two days if I moved quickly. I was not happy about the direction they took because that was the territory where there were a lot of Ukrainian Guerillas who were fighting for the Germans. I had no choice but to follow them as I could not make it all the way by myself. I started out in that same direction. I rode all day and night. I stopped the next day only for a few minutes to give the horses some rest but continued right away. Suddenly, I heard shooting. I was petrified and paralyzed with fear. I had no idea what to do. In my heart, I knew my boys were involved in this fight, but on the other hand, I could not be sure. I hurried up and started to move in the direction of the shooting. When I got close, I put the horses under cover and picked a position from where I could oversee the territory.

A chill went through my body like a cold, deadly wind through my bones. I spotted the two wagons in the middle of a field, surrounded by about thirty men on horses and on foot firing at them with everything they had. Here again, all by myself, I had to think of a plan. My first reaction was to take the horses and leave in another direction so that at least I would make it out alive, but all of a sudden, I felt as though I had awakened from a long sleep and could not believe that those thoughts had crossed my mind. I was the only chance those boys had to survive. If I left, there would be nothing left of them. I sat down and thought about what I could do to help them. I wanted to wait until dark, hoping that by then, I would be able to reach them, or another Russian patrol would come along and chase the others away. This was not a good plan because my friends could easily run out of ammunition by then. I returned to the bushes and picked a site about two hundred feet long.

I then collected about two hundred hand grenades I found in the fields that the Germans and Russians left. I even found some artillery shrapnel shells that I could use as explosives. I distributed them in a line and connected them with a wire and a fuse. When I ignited the first one, the fire went down the line, causing an explosion every second. With all the explosions, an old barn also caught on fire. When the attackers heard the noise I had caused, they immediately pulled back. I then mounted my horse and rode out into the open. My group started to fire, but it was on me this time. I yelled at the top of my lungs for them to stop shooting that it was me, the Little General. They recognized me, immediately ceased fire, and came to greet me. They were ecstatic to see me.

CHAPTER 13:

Full Circle

Once again, it was a happy reunion. Situations like these always reminded me of my dear Irka and our happy reunions. The Officer also came up to me and kissed me. He told me that if we returned to camp, he would immediately appoint me as an officer and nominate me for the biggest Russian award. As all the men were starved, I distributed food and drink to everyone. By drink, I do not mean water. I brought plenty of Vodka that I had loaded onto the horse when I left the wagon behind. This Vodka was a crucial part of my survival. I did not quite understand it, but it gave me great courage. Everyone received a generous drink of Vodka. When dark settled upon us, we moved on to find a safer place to camp for the night. We all needed some rest after the day of fighting. We traveled about ten miles until we found the right spot to set up camp.

The next morning, we started out early. We had to find another wagon because three of us were badly wounded. We arrived at a small village and looked for another wagon to be pulled by one of my extra horses. Unfortunately, the bandits that had attacked us the previous day occupied this village, so not only did they refuse to give us anything, but also one of them fired a shot and killed one of our men. This was too much for us. We surrounded the village and set it on fire. We threw in all the ammunition we had and almost used up all our hand grenades. We had to make sure that no one would escape. We treated them the same as they would have treated us. I did, however, make sure that there were no women or children in this village before we set it on fire. After this attack, we headed out to return to the camp. We were close and figured it would take another day or two to get there. Before setting the village on fire, we took a dozen horses and plenty of food. We loaded everything on the extra wagons and rode all day. When it got dark, we set up camp in a place where there was sufficient cover in case of an ambush.

We moved out early the next morning. After riding for about thirty miles, we met another group of ours that had just started on the same journey we were returning from. We got together and shared our stories. The group warned us that the day before, they had a big fight with some Germans cut off from their outfits and more German units were running around. We gave each other useful advice and continued on our way.

We traveled all day without trouble and could do good mileage because we had fresh horses and were well-rested. We arrived at our last resting place before reaching our camp. We all went to sleep excitedly, knowing we would reach camp the next day. No one expected what happened next. We woke up the next morning to the sight of Germans surrounding us. There were German soldiers everywhere. We could not even see a tree in the forest, just Germans. We huddled together closely and worked out a plan quickly. Because we could not run, everyone grabbed hold of a rifle, climbed up a tree, and began to fire at anything that moved. Our sick boys who could not climb fired from the ground. This was the best tactic for us because the fire from the ground level pushed the Germans back. Once the Germans started moving back, we slid down from the trees and chased them out of the woods. They ran so fast that they looked like a herd of deer. When the fighting calmed down, and the shooting stopped, we searched the area to see if they had left anything behind. The Germans always left something behind. Sure enough, we found a lot of stuff to load onto the wagons. By noontime, we were ready to head out again. This time, we did not stop, nor did we have any intentions to stop, anywhere until we got back to our camp. We finally reached our camp at three o'clock in the morning.

It was a beautiful spring morning when we arrived at camp. Everything was turning green again. We entered quietly, not to wake anyone, and went straight to sleep. After several hours of sleep, we were awakened by an alarm because some Germans had been spotted in our neighborhood. The scout patrol reported that they had observed an entire German army group heading straight to our camp from the same direction from which we had come. We figured these Germans had followed us all the way, but we had made it back faster because we were on horses. This time, we were ready to give them a big reception.

Our camp had about one thousand people, of which approximately ninety percent were armed. We also had plenty of light artillery. We took positions and waited for orders to open fire. We counted about a thousand German soldiers, but they were exhausted from marching all night. We took them by surprise. After half an hour, the battle ended. There were about three hundred dead Germans, and the rest we took as prisoners. We did not have the space to hold seven hundred prisoners, so all we could do was mobilize several local farmers and turn them over to them until the Russian army arrived, which we had estimated to be in about three days at the latest.

That same day, our Commissar Commander gave us a big reception and called me out of the line, announcing that I was a company leader from now on. He then assigned one hundred men to me. This position did not last long because about a week later, the Russian Army arrived and released us from all combat duty. Everyone received two weeks' leave except for all Russian citizens who had to report to the regular Russian army immediately and were sent into combat moving toward Germany. After our two weeks' rest, all non-Russian citizens were assigned to the police force to clean out the Ukrainian Guerillas that were fighting against us. This assignment lasted about two months, keeping us moving from place to place until an order came from Moscow that all Polish citizens were to return to their hometowns.

Once again, I arrived at my hometown by train. We had to walk about three miles from the railroad station to my town. I remembered the last time I walked along this road was with my father and about ten thousand other Jewish people, being chased along by SS guards destined for liquidation. I recalled I had been fortunate enough to escape that time, but I did not think I was fortunate at this moment because I had no idea where I was going or what I would find. Every step I took reminded me of another unhappy, tragic event. I had to continue, to see for myself what was left of this beautiful place where I had once been so happy.

I was carrying nothing except the clothes on my back. All the while, I was setting one foot in front of the other, almost in a mechanical way, recognizing every stone, tree, and corner of my town. There were few houses left in the Jewish part of town. I walked all over town the entire day, trying to remember how beautiful everything had been before. Beautiful memories came to mind but were immediately interrupted by recent unhappy events. I walked over to where my house had been and quickly realized that it was gone. After the Germans had liquidated the town, they burned down the entire Jewish Ghetto.

I then headed to the Jewish Cemetery to see if I could find the graves of my family. All I could find was one large grave containing about five hundred bodies. I could not believe that there, among those hundreds of bodies thrown into this so-called grave, were my parents and grandparents. I sat down for a while and thought about my family. I thought of each of them, my mother, father, sister, brother, and my dear grandparents. Why weren't some of them here? Why could I not see them? What good people they were. Why could I not see them again? If only I could see them one more time, even for a little while. I cried and cried. Once again, I was alone. The only one left from my entire family. I had to get up and leave this place once and for all, knowing that I would never return.

I walked straight back to the train station. I waited all night for a train to arrive and carry me away. I could not bear this town any longer. I boarded the first train, pulling into the station, not knowing where it was headed and not caring either. I just wanted to get away. I just wanted to forget. It took me many years to get over everything, and right now, as I am writing this book, all the memories still come back, causing me to cry just as much as I did then. It is difficult for me to write all of this down, but I have to do it because even today, many people are unaware of all these things that occurred and could benefit from reading about my experience. Whoever reads this story should know that this is a real-life story, full of sweat, tears, and blood.

There I was on a train, but to where I did not know. The first station was Sobibor. Sobibor was the concentration camp in which I worked for about six months and where my life almost ended. The train stopped there for about ten minutes, and in those ten minutes, I relived all the terrible things that had happened to me at this camp. The train then started to move. After about five hours, we arrived at Chelm. Once again, my memories came back connected with this town and little beautiful Sara, who was dead too. All she wanted was to live and love, but nothing was left. We travelled deeper into the country's center.

After one week on that train, with almost no food or water, the train arrived in Warsaw, the capital of Poland. It was about two o'clock in the morning, and no living soul was seen at the station. All I could see around me were the ruins. I found a place in the ruins to lie down and rest for the night. I could still hear artillery fire and airplanes flying back and forth all night. The next day, I started to walk. I had no idea where I was going because this was the first time I had ever been to Warsaw. I walked around all day. All I saw were Russian and Polish soldiers. Finally, at night, I saw some civilians and asked them if they knew of any place I could find shelter. They gave me the address of a Red Cross station, but I would have to wait until the following morning to go there. They were kind enough to give me things to eat and drink. It did not take long for a Polish Patrol to come along and look me over. They asked me how old I was, and I answered I was fourteen, which made me too young for the army but not too young to be put to work.

Once again, I was a prisoner. The war was definitely not over yet. They took me to a work camp inhabited only by young people, and all we did was dig ditches along the front lines. At least we had some food, drink, and shelter. I was there for three months. Several of the children were killed by artillery fire during work. It did not take me long to realize this was no place for me, and I had to get out of there as quickly as possible. I escaped the camp and moved behind the front lines to a German city called Stettin. There, I immediately located the Jewish office, and for the first time since I left home, I was treated like a human being again.

CHAPTER 14:

No End in Sight

It was close to the end of the war, and every day, more Jewish people from all over Europe poured into Stettin. Initially, I acted like a social worker, helping new arrivals, but because I was not used to sitting in one place for long, I found something else to do. Immediately after the war, a new underground movement was formed in Poland to fight the Communist government.

These new underground organizations used the same tactics as the Nazis to eliminate the Jews. Every day, there were new victims. They wiped out entire Jewish families, and no one did anything about it. I rounded up several veterans like me, and we patrolled the area every night but were not having much luck catching up with them.

One night, as everyone was sleeping, I awoke to some strange sounds next door. I woke up the rest of the group and went out to see what was causing the commotion. A large Jewish family from Russia had just moved in next door. There were about a dozen of those Nazi cooperators in that house trying to force the family out, to take them out of town and shoot them one by one. We grabbed our arms and surprised these dirty invaders by jumping them. Fortunately, they did not resist us, so we threw them on their truck, took them to the first police station, and turned them over to the authorities.

The police did not do a thing about them. The next day, those men were walking freely around town. It appeared we could do nothing about it.

Shortly after this incident, a large-scale exodus began from Poland to West Germany. Most people found refuge in the so-called U.N.R.A. (UN Relief Agency) camps; from there, every man was on his own. This is when I started the first profitable business of my life. Although it was a risky one, I made enough money to maintain our operations. I bought trucks from officers of the Russian Army and used these trucks as transportation for the refugees.

We carried forty people at a time. Half of the people would pay for the service, and the other half who were too poor rode for free. A friend and I dressed in Russian officer uniforms and drove away with all those people, including women and children.

Along the way, we passed several Polish, Russian, and East German guards for about two hundred and fifty miles until we reached West Berlin. In Berlin, we took the people to the U.N.R.A. camps or the Jewish American Organization called JOINT. We used to make these trips once a month, and then the word got out, and more people started the same operation.

These trips were no picnics but were exceptionally successful. We were fortunate because many other people had bad luck and were cut off by the Russians or East Germans. They were arrested and kept in jail for a long time or shipped to Russia.

One day, I tired of all of this and thought that because I had lived through so much danger in the past, now that the war was over, there was no reason I should keep risking my life. I went back to Poland to take care of a few personal matters first, and then wanted to return to West Germany - to Berlin, to plan a new life. In Stettin I had an apartment and a lot of friends. One night though, about two weeks later, a Russian Patrol picked me up and threw me into jail.

For two weeks, they kept me there without food, and I had no clue where I was. They questioned me and accused me of being an American spy. Every night for a month, they hauled me from jail and interrogated me. They wanted to know from whom I was receiving orders. Of course, they got nothing out of me. Finally, one night, a Russian officer appeared and recited a long list of offenses and sentenced me to twenty years of hard labor in Siberia for treason. That same night, they put me on a train to Siberia.

I was completely alone and locked up in a freight train boxcar. All I had were two pounds of bread and a jar of water. I can only remember when the train started to move; after that, I do not know how long I traveled because I lost count of the days. The train made many stops, and I never knew where I was; all I knew was that it was getting colder every day.

The entire trip took about a month. All I had to eat the entire trip was what they had given me in Poland, which lasted for three days. The rest of the days, I ate what I could scrape from the walls of the box car and drank rainwater or sucked on the ice that formed in the car. The four weeks that trip lasted felt like four years. I could not believe this was happening to me.

After everything I had been through, everything I had survived, it was impossible for me to grasp that something like this was happening. I was convinced that I had lost my mind completely and could not think clearly anymore. At that point, I truly lost hope and did not care what would happen to me or where they were taking me. The only human contact I had during that month was a man who came outside my car daily, called out my name until I answered, and left until the following day to perform the same duty.

After four weeks on this train, the doors of my boxcar opened for the first time, and for the first time in weeks, I saw sun and daylight. Everything was hazy, and I became dizzy. A few men in uniforms, which I did not recognize, led me to a car that drove us about five blocks. Because I was so weak and could not walk, I had to be carried into the house, which seemed to be a police station. They gave me hot water and bread. This was my first meal in four weeks. Two guards then led me out of the room. I had no idea where I was or where they were taking me.

It was freezing outside, and I had no winter clothes, so I had to move around to keep myself warm. The guards were dressed in heavy winter coats and wore Walonki, a type of wool boots. We walked for an entire day and finally reached a camp. I was told to gather wood for a fire. One of the guards handed me a pound of black bread and told me to eat. I was so happy they had given me the bread because I was about to faint from starvation. I warmed up some water to drink. This was my first dinner in Siberia.

After dinner, one guard went to sleep, and the other watched over me as if I even knew where I was and where to run. It did not even make a difference to me; I no longer cared about anything that was going on. At that point, I could not have cared less if the entire world had vanished. There was no way I could sleep because of the severe cold. Even if I could have fallen asleep, I would have frozen to death with what I was wearing, so I walked around in circles the entire night trying to keep a little warmer.

We started out again early the next morning. We had to move slowly because I was so weak and could hardly walk. Fortunately, the guards did not push me too hard, and I could sense they actually felt sorry for me. At around three o'clock in the afternoon, we arrived at a place that was in the middle of nowhere.

All I saw was a river and something that resembled a booth. The guards then turned me over to two other guards already waiting for me in the booth. The journey then continued. The new guards led the way. Again, I did not know where I was or where I was going. All I wanted was another pound of bread. The guards gave me a fresh ration of half a pound of bread and told me that if I wanted to drink, I would have to drink from the river. We journeyed down the river on a barge for about a week. They gave me less and less bread to eat every day. For the last two days, there was no bread at all. All I had was the water in the river.

When we arrived at our destination, I was shocked at what I saw. It looked exactly like a concentration camp, but this time, it was in Russia, not Germany. It had barbed wire surrounding it and a dozen dilapidated barracks for the prisoners. Everything around the camp was bare.

A Russian officer greeted us at the camp and released the two other guards. The officer led me into the guardhouse and read me a few lines from a paper, of which I did not understand one word, but he was the boss, so I listened. I was told right away that I was not permitted to talk to anyone and that all I should do was follow orders. I was then assigned to a barrack. This was my first day as a prisoner in a Russian concentration camp in Siberia, in the middle of absolutely nowhere.

Our barrack was about one hundred feet long by twenty-five feet wide, was built from single boards of lumber, and had no floor, just bare ground. Benches stacked in twos served as bunks and were lined up in two rows. This barrack, as well as the others in the camp, housed mostly German POWs. I knew what to expect from them. I assumed that many of them had belonged to the SS or Gestapo, so I made sure not to tell anyone I was Jewish. Here, once again, I had to hide that I was Jewish.

I introduced myself to the other prisoners as a Volksdeutscher (a German living outside the German borders) from Poland, informing them that I could speak neither German nor Russian, only Polish.

There were many more young German boys like me. I attached myself to the young ones because the Russians did not assign such hard work to them.

The first time I lined up for the morning appellation, we were called out by numbers, not names. As far as I can remember, my number was thirteen hundred. After everyone answered by number, we were on our way to work. We walked for about an hour deep into the woods. We cut down timber in large pieces, dragged it to the river, pushed it in, and let it float downstream. My work was the same as the other prisoners my age.

We had to gather all the branches, put them in one pile, and then light them on fire. I worked like this for about two months or more; I had lost track of time, so I am unsure. All I could think about every day was how I would get out of there. However, I could not come up with a plan whatsoever.

There was nothing to help me figure out how to escape in the least bit. I had no indication of which direction to take because there was no traffic in and around the camp; no one came and left. Dozens of people died every day from starvation and the extreme cold. Once a day, we received a bowl of soup, but it was not regular soup; it was plain water with cabbage leaves and one slice of bread.

After the third month of hell, I finally got a break. Some downstream timber had piled up and blocked the river about fifty miles from camp. Along with a dozen others, I was selected to walk to that place, accompanied by two guards, and move the timber that had piled up. It took us three days to reach the area. I noticed that there was a nearby village with about one hundred inhabitants.

The first night after our arrival, I snuck away, unnoticed by the guards, and entered the village. All I could find out was that this place was about two thousand miles from Moscow and that a car would come bringing mail and supplies for the nearby villages every three months. I asked them for food and was given some potatoes and bread. Unfortunately, that was all they could spare because they hardly had enough food for themselves. When I told them I was a Jew and that I was imprisoned together with Germans, they felt sorry for me and tried to help me as much as they could.

I snuck away from the guards every night and went into the village.

After several visits, the people came to like me and started to prepare specially cooked meals for me. They begged me to tell them about life in Poland, so I told them about my country and childhood. They liked me more and more.

After every story I told them, they expressed their disbelief at how good people lived in Poland and other European countries. I told them stories of the war and how the Jews lived through the German occupation, which seemed completely unbelievable to them. Eventually, they decided to help me get back home.

After working there for a month, we still had plenty of work to do because there was more timber piling up every day. One night, when I came to the village, the people anxiously awaited me because they had good news to tell me. One of them invited me into his house and told me that if I was still thinking of running away, now was the time.

They had a man with horses willing to take me to the nearest city, but we would have to ride for about four days through the tundra, large swamps, and deep woods. I immediately accepted the offer. There was no time to waste.

They had everything ready for the journey.

I was on my way again to Liberty. The man who accompanied me, Igor, was about thirty years old, single, slim, and even though he had never attended school, he was intelligent. He had chosen to help me because he wanted to get away from this place just as badly as I wanted to. We agreed he would take me out of Siberia, and I would take him along wherever I would go. I was more than happy to do so.

CHAPTER 15:

Journey to Liberty

The first night with Igor was the first night that I slept warmly because he held me in his arms all night, just as a mother holds their child. When Igor woke me up the next morning, he gave me a little to eat, and then we mounted our horses and continued on our way. We rode through tall and deep forests. I had never seen such tall, large trees; all covered in snow. Everything was so strangely silent. The silence took my happiness away from being liberated. The only thing that comforted me was the beautiful, clear blue sky shining through the treetops. Ever since then, blue has been my favorite color.

Igor became everything to me. He was now my mother, my father, and my friend. Never again did I find someone like him. He was calculated and thought carefully about every possible situation. Luckily, he knew the territory very well. He decided to leave the horses so we could travel by canoe for a while and then continue on foot. The canoe ride ended up being quite beautiful. The weather was a bit cold, and because we were running short on food, we were able to catch some fish. That was the best dinner I had had in years. Our canoe ride ended the next day, and it was time to travel on foot. We were now in the middle of nowhere. We walked along a trail that led us to railroad tracks. After several hours of walking, I noticed a house with smoke coming out of the chimney in the distance, which led us to believe people were living there. The only problem was that we had no idea who these people were and if they would be friends or foes. The police might have been already looking for us. We decided not to take any chances and changed direction to bypass the house unnoticed. It was getting dark by now, so we looked for a place to sleep for the night. Luckily, there was no snow there because spring had arrived. We ate some leftover fish from the night before and had a good night's sleep.

The following day, we moved right along and reached the railroad tracks. As we walked closer, we noticed a nearby village.

This time, it was a large village. All we could think about was food, but we decided to wait until dark to be able to walk around without being noticed. Once it was dark enough, we entered the village. There were a few people on the streets. We picked the first house at the village entrance and knocked on the door. A woman's voice answered, "Shto we Hatitie?" Igor replied, "Pakusiat Babushka." The door opened, and an old woman appeared. Igor kneeled in front of her and prayed. There was not much in the house because it had only one room.

Most of the Russian houses were like this. A large stone oven stood in the middle of the room, like an old-fashioned bakery oven. The house did not have a kitchen, only this stove, which was used for cooking, baking, and sleeping on at night; they called it a Pechka. A little fire burned in the oven, and one pot containing potatoes simmered on it. The old lady said she would be glad to share her potatoes with us, but unfortunately, there was not enough for all of us. Igor walked out for a few minutes and then returned with a whole bushel of potatoes. We put them in the oven and baked them until they were brown. This was a wonderful dinner; we even had leftovers to take with us for the next day. Igor asked the old lady all kinds of questions. She said that about one hundred soldiers on horses passed through the village a few days prior. They had stopped and announced that they were looking for some German prisoners who had escaped the prison camp and that everyone had to report immediately to the eldest of the village if they noticed any strangers. Everyone in the village was on the lookout for these strangers. The old lady proceeded to tell us we had nothing to worry about because we were not Germans, and no one would harm us. We decided not to take any chances, and early the next morning, while the Babushka was still asleep, we left the house.

We were off again on our journey to Liberty. We walked along the tracks until we reached a spot where the tracks went uphill. Igor found a place to hide until a train passed onto which we could jump. We found a convenient place to hide. We waited twenty-four hours, and there was still no sign of a train. We had nothing to eat, so Igor went back to the village and returned with food that would last for about two days.

We waited for another two days and still no train. Early the next morning, we heard a train approaching, but unfortunately, it was heading in the opposite direction. We were back at square one. We waited for three more days, but nothing happened. I lost my patience and suggested to Igor to keep moving on foot. Igor did not agree with me; he considered it much too dangerous to walk because from now on, we would reach more densely populated areas, and there would be more police around. Naturally, to go ahead would be asking for trouble, so I agreed to stay and wait until a train came.

Two days later, once again, we heard a train approaching. As it came closer, we noticed it was headed in the right direction this time. We got ready to jump, not to lose a second when the train passed. The train came so we waited for the last car. Just as we had anticipated, the train slowed down considerably when it started going uphill, and we jumped. We made it without any problems and now were on our way again.

We entered the train's last car and started to pay attention to the land passing by to orient ourselves to where we were. The car we rode in was empty. The train rolled for about twenty-four hours until it stopped to load some water. This was our opportunity to climb out and look for something to eat. We could not spare much time, so we had to hurry. There were no houses around, only the refueling station. We headed back to the train and continued without any food. We took turns sleeping so that one of us could always stand watch in case the train would stop again. After another twenty-four hours, the train stopped. It was the middle of the night, so we could not see a thing; we jumped down from the train and looked around. Igor spotted a small house. As we got closer, we realized this was not a house but a depot. We did not waste any time, and Igor broke in. He did not stay long but came out with a sack over his shoulders. We took plenty of water and hopped back on the train with our new findings. When we entered the train, we immediately opened the sack to find nothing but packages of white powder. At first, because we did not know what it was, we were disappointed. I opened a package and tasted it.

To my surprise, it was dry milk. We mixed the powder with water and were able to enjoy the milk. I still remember to this day how delicious that milk tasted. It lasted for two days.

The train stopped after three more days of travel and twenty-four hours without food or water. This time we were in a big town. It was nighttime, so the streets were empty. As we were looking out of the car, we noticed they were separating our car from the rest of the train. Igor made the wise decision to remain in the car overnight and explore the town in the morning because sneaking around at night surely would have raised suspicions.

We rested all night and woke up early in the morning. We looked out of the car and saw people walking in the streets. Everyone seemed to be going to work. There were a lot of men, women, and teenagers. We got out of the car and moved into the crowd, not knowing where we were headed. We followed the traffic and arrived at a big gate, which was the entrance of a factory. We could not walk into the factory, so we turned around and headed back. I overheard two men, who were walking ahead, talking about us. I was sure they were talking about us because they mentioned an escape from Siberia and that the police were already on the tracks of the escapees.

We felt completely helpless; we had no idea what to do. We kept walking until we lost the two men. We headed out of the town immediately. After walking for quite some time, a police car pulled up in front of us and asked us for our papers. We had no papers, so they took us down to the station. We were devastated. We thought this was the end of our journey to Liberty. They kept us seated at the station all day without asking us even one question. I could no longer stand our fate's uncertainty and burst into tears. The officer came out of his room. I told him that I was German and could not speak Russian. He came back with an old man who spoke German. The minute the old man opened his mouth, I noticed he could not speak a word of German, but he spoke Yiddish. I told him that I was not German but a Jewish boy from Poland. He did not believe me at first.

He asked me a few questions about Poland and what city I came from. I answered him freely, and he told me he was also from Poland. He calmed me down and told me not to worry, as he would do everything he could to help me. He left the room for a few minutes and returned with food for us both. I then told him the rest of my story. After hearing my story, the old man left for about two hours and returned with a few other Jewish people. They reassured us that everything would end well and not to worry. They all left the police station for the night but promised to return first thing in the morning to take us out of there.

The next morning, the same group returned just as they had promised. They brought us food and then walked straight into the Commissar's room. We had no idea what was going on there, so all I did was pray and pray hard. It sounded as though they were bargaining. Suddenly, the group of Jews came out of the room and told us we were free to go and that we should come with them. We immediately left the station and walked about thirty blocks until we arrived at a big house that looked like a school. In the house were hundreds of men, women, and children. They were all Jews from Poland. They were waiting in the house for transportation back to Poland because immediately after the war, Russia passed a law that all Polish citizens must return to their homeland. They gave us papers to enable us to walk around town freely. From this point on, Igor was no longer Russian. Igor was now a Jew, and he was happy about it.

CHAPTER 16.

A Different Course

We stayed in this school for about two months until a train arrived with more Polish citizens. This time, there were many Gentiles among them. We all were given a ration of food that would last about one week and then proceeded to board the train. We were on our way again, but this time to Poland. The train advanced slowly because it would stop at every station for two or three days, so our food ran out before we reached our destination. We had traveled only about two hundred miles and were already starving. We had an older man on the train who was responsible for us. At the next stop, our elder walked into town with a few others to see the Commissar of that town and to request food. The Commissar told them that the Polish office in the next town was already expecting us, and we would get everything we needed there. The only problem was that while we were waiting for the elder to return from the Commissar, the locomotive had been detached from our train, and we could not get to the next town where the food awaited us. After waiting four days, someone got a hold of a messenger willing to ride to the next town, which would take about twenty-four hours, to advise the Polish officials of our situation. This messenger asked for money, but unfortunately, no one had any. We decided that some women would have to give up their wedding rings. Two of the women volunteered and gave their rings to the messenger. He then mounted his horse and headed out.

We knew we would have to wait for at least two days to hear from the messenger, and in the meantime, we all were starving. Igor and I decided to take a walk and see what we could do about the situation. We encountered a large pile of frozen potatoes about three miles from our train. We filled our pockets and went back to the train. We passed on the word where the potatoes were located, and everyone ran out to get some. By the time they arrived at the pile, guards had already been posted. Everyone was so hungry that they did not care about the guards. Guard or no guard, they wanted something to eat. They stormed the guards and the pile. The guards did not take this lightly and opened fire on everyone and killed six people, all because they had taken a few frozen potatoes. Four men and two women were killed, and no one cared. More guards arrived and forced everyone back onto the train. If anyone tried to stick his head out of the car, he was shot at instantly. For two days, we were held prisoners on the train. Finally, the messenger returned accompanied by a representative of the Polish government. He called us all together and announced that several wagons with all the food we needed would arrive in the morning. He calmed us all down. We all returned to our places on the train and waited for morning. No one could sleep. We all were starving.

Just as the man had told us, in the morning the food wagons arrived. We all got into a line and waited for our turn to receive our food ration. The Polish representative ensured a locomotive was sent and hitched up to the train so we could be on our way to Poland. We traveled day and night for another four lonely weeks, only stopping for water and other vital needs. We finally made it to the Russian/Polish border. We all had to get off the train to cross the border on foot.

We were once again in Poland. No matter how badly I wanted to forget the past few years and escape those memories, I kept ending up in that same place. It seemed as though I would never be able to leave and forget my past. As soon as I crossed the border, everything came to my mind again: all that had happened to my family. I still could not believe that I would never see my family again. It seemed like a bad dream. Because I was with so many people all the time, I would stare at their faces, hoping to find someone in my family among them. I would look at every face, trying to recognize someone. I finally asked myself why I was doing this when I knew for a fact that my entire family had been killed. Why was I torturing myself like that? Eventually, I stopped looking.

When it was my turn to pass the Polish border control, I could not state my real name, so I made one up, and everything went fine. The procedure at the border control lasted all day.

At night, we were already on the Polish side, and there were several people from a local Jewish organization waiting for us with food and medical supplies. They attended to the sick, children, and women first. We were then led to a nearby small town and placed in a large house for the night. Later that same night, we suddenly heard shots being fired. We had no idea what was going on and became alarmed and panicked. I pushed myself through the crowd as I tried to make my way out, but it was impossible because our building was under heavy fire from the outside. I asked a few young boys standing beside me if they would like to join me and try to get out of the house to see what was happening. They agreed to join me. When the shots quieted down, two of us left the house through the rear door. I looked around every corner of the house, and as far as I could see, there was a group of ten wild Polish Gentile boys holding five people from our house hostage. I saw them undress the people and shoot them on the spot. I could not just sit and watch this but did not know what to do. I did not have any weapons to shoot with, so I started to scream hysterically, as loud as I could. My screaming startled the Polish boys, so they turned around and started shooting at me, but luckily, I was well covered. While they were focusing all their firing on me, the rest of the people in the house ran out into the streets, screaming and shouting and scaring the bandits away. I could not believe that the war was over, and we were still dealing with this terrible anti-Semitism.

The following day, I decided to break away from the group and go on my own. The Jewish people who received us at the border had given us one thousand Zloty, which equaled approximately twenty US Dollars. I began my journey. I walked for about thirty days, from farm to farm, begging for food until I reached a train station. I entered one of the cars, not knowing where I was headed and not caring because at least I was headed somewhere. I was so exhausted from all the walking that I fell asleep immediately. As I was sleeping, the train moved out. The train stopped only after forty-eight hours. I decided to continue on foot because we were stopped for over twenty-four hours. After I began to walk, I noticed the train could not have gone any further because a bridge up ahead was destroyed. As I walked, I came across signs on the road with names of little towns, but none looked familiar. Finally, after several hours, I saw a sign that read "Warsaw 250 Kilometers."

I finally knew where I was and how long it would take to get somewhere. I hitched rides along the way and arrived in Warsaw in two days.

I immediately located the office of the Jewish Organization. When I arrived at their office, it was different from the others. By now, many people had gathered from Russian and German concentration camps, and they had set up something similar to a Kibbutz. A Kibbutz is a collective community in Israel that combines Socialism and Zionism. Everyone at this camp was preparing for immigration to our Jewish land, Israel. It was a small Exodus. This was all new to me. Every now and then, a few lucky people were chosen for an illegal trip to Israel. I was never picked. After several weeks, I decided that my fate was in my hands and that it would be better for me to plan my own trip. Here I was again, on my way, like the other trips I had made. The only difference was that this time, I had a goal. This time, I knew where I wanted to go. This time, it was a trip to a place where I could make a home, a place where I would be expected.

I went straight to the central railroad station and bought a ticket to Stettin, the German city annexed to Poland after the war. I immediately boarded the train. Although it was not yet departure time, the train was already heavily occupied, and there was only standing room left. Even the halls and platforms of the train were crowded. After standing in the same spot on the train for several hours, my feet became tired, and I was extremely sleepy. I had to find a place to lie down, but every inch of the car as well as the outside platform was crowded with people. I noticed a lot of people going in and out of the toilet room, so I took my place in the line.

When it was my turn, I entered the toilet room, locked the door, sat down, and fell asleep. I was so tired that I did not care about the people knocking on the door waiting to use the toilet and continued to sleep. I woke up in the morning to the stench of the toilet. I smelled so bad that everyone turned away as I exited the toilet room. Smelling like this, I traveled for two more days until we arrived in Stettin. I immediately looked for the Jewish organization again. It was late at night when I arrived at the office, so I found a place to sleep nearby.

In the morning, I went to the office and registered as a refugee, which entitled me to room and board and a few Zloty.

CHAPTER 17:

Changes on the Horizon

Here, for the first time in years, I felt free. I finally had a place to come home to. I stayed at a refugee center for Jewish people who came from all over Russia and Poland and were waiting for immigration to Israel, America, Australia, and South America. People wanted to go to wherever they had relatives who had migrated before the war. Unfortunately, we could not leave Poland freely, so the only alternative was to do it illegally, which was close to impossible. Few could afford to pay large sums of money to the border officials to let them pass through during the night. Many people were so desperate that they were cheated of their life savings. They were promised free passage, and then after they had paid, they were arrested for spying and never came back from the police station. Everything was a risk and a dangerous risk. After many failed bribery attempts, one man devised a plan. The plan was to organize a group of young men like me and to figure out a way to bring as many people as possible from Poland to Germany, where they had established a so-called DP camp (Displaced Persons camp). Once you arrived at the DP camp, you can travel anywhere in the world. Within three days, about twenty men, including myself, were selected for this job.

We sat up every night for one week trying to devise a plan and arrived at the only feasible solution. We planned to steal trucks from the Russian and Polish armies stationed in Poland close to Stettin. We began the operation immediately. I was the only one who could drive a truck, so I became the chauffeur. I searched throughout the day to locate a truck and, at midnight, went back and drove off with it. The actual stealing of the car took about five minutes. All the trucks, mostly GMC, Ford, and Dodge, were manufactured in America. I drove straight to the Jewish Center and loaded sixty to seventy men, women, and children.

When I approached the border, I slowed down because a guard stood in the middle of the road. Once I was at a halt, the guard approached my window and asked me for identification. I was dressed in uniform, so he suspected nothing.

He was convinced that I was some high-ranking Russian officer. When the guard was close enough, I opened the truck door, kicked him down with my foot, and stepped on the gas pedal. At a fast speed, I crashed through the barrier and made it to the German side. Even though we were on the German side, we were still not safe because it was East German territory, and we could be stopped at any time. I drove as fast as possible because we still had a two-hour drive until we were safe. Luckily, everything went smoothly; by six in the morning, we had reached the American sector of Berlin, where the DP camp was located. We were welcomed there with open arms and were given all the help we needed. I turned the truck over to the local Jewish organization, being that I had no use for it anymore. We then all registered with the camp, which was called Schlachtensee.

After a long rest in Berlin, I received a message from my friends in Poland to return because many people were waiting for me. I packed up and started my journey back to Poland without any valid papers. This would not be an easy task. I had to pass through the Russian zone in Germany with hundreds of control points that the Russians and Germans manned. The only way I could travel was by train. The only form of identification I had was a card that I was issued at the DP camp; however, if I were to present that card to any of the authorities, I would be immediately arrested as a spy. I realized that I had a letter with me written by the Jewish Community in Hebrew, with many signatures and seals on it. I presented this document to Russian control. Thank goodness it worked. The Russians would walk through the cars at every train stop and request identification. I handed them the letter and every time, they seemed puzzled by it. Each guard would examine it, turn it around, then turn it again, and still could not understand a word. By the time the train gave the signal to pull out, they had still not figured it out. The train would start to roll, and they would give the letter back to me and jump off. I could make it back to Poland safely, all because of this letter.

When I arrived in Stettin, everyone was thrilled to see me and ready to leave. They already had a truck filled with passengers waiting for me. I explained to them that there was no way I would leave that night.

I had to get some rest and wanted to double-check the situation at the border to make sure of any changes. The next day, a couple of friends and I drove to the border in a private car to look around. Everything seemed to be okay; however, I wanted to be one hundred percent sure. I approached the guard with the excuse that I had lost my dog and asked if he had seen him. As I got closer to the guard, I recognized him. The guard was an old friend of mine named Marek. During the war, we fought together in the Partisan group. Marek could not believe his eyes. He was overwhelmed with joy. We started talking about old times, and he told me he was the only guard on duty from midnight until morning. I could not believe how perfect this was. I felt as though he had been sent to me from above. I began to talk business with him. At first, he did not like the idea, but he consented when I offered him one thousand dollars every time he would let us pass. I loaded the truck that night, and we were on our way to Germany. It was like taking a simple ride after dinner. We arrived at Schlachtenasee, the DP camp in Berlin without any problem.

Due to this excellent opportunity, I could not lose any time, so I drove back to Poland for another pick-up. Just as before, there was another truck waiting for me. Before taking the passengers, I went to the border to confirm that Marek would be on duty that evening. That same night, I loaded the truck and drove to Berlin. I continued these missions for almost two months, transporting refugees three to four times a week. On a usual trip to Berlin, one night, I was stopped by a German patrol. When I looked out my window, I noticed they had surrounded us. As expected, all the women and children on the truck started to cry hysterically and panicked. My only option was to make a run for it. I took off as fast as I could while the Germans chased after me in the American jeeps that they had received from the Russians. Even though I was driving as fast as I could get the engine to go, the Germans were still following and firing at us. Suddenly, the Germans shot one of my tires, and I lost control. I immediately ordered everyone to jump off, but some were too scared and stayed on the truck. I stuck to the wheel until the truck skidded into a ditch and overturned.

I was unconscious for a few minutes and when I came to, I noticed about one hundred Germans were swarming all over the place, yelling, "Juden, Juden." The worst part was when I realized that six people were smashed under the truck. I got up slowly and asked the nearest German for their officer. I surprised them by telling them I was a Russian officer and had now lost my papers due to the accident. I then asked him if he could give me a few of his officers to help me erect the truck and pick up the wounded. He respected my wishes and ordered a few of them to help me. The wounded were put on a German truck and taken to a nearby hospital. Two of the wounded recovered. Right after the accident, a few more Germans and Russians arrived.

They rounded us all up, loaded us one by one on their trucks, and took us to the nearest town, which was about twenty-five miles away. We were then booked into a jail, and all thrown into one room. We were kept in this jail for three days without being asked a single question or given any food. We shared whatever food we had been able to rescue from the accident and take with us. On the third day, they began questioning us separately. This went on for another two days. When they were finished with their questioning, they called us all into a large room, similar to a courtroom, and read us our sentences. All of the women and children were sent back to Poland, some of the men were sent away to an unknown location, and the rest of us were sentenced to jail terms from one to five years to be served in a jail in Poland. We were then loaded onto trucks and shipped out in different directions. As we approached the Polish border, I offered the Russian guard my watch as a bribe to let me jump off the truck. I knew this was extremely risky because there was a big chance he would take the watch, let me jump, and then shoot me as soon as I hit the ground. I had no other option but to take this chance. He accepted the watch, and without thinking much longer, I jumped. Luckily, he did not shoot me.

I knew I had to get back to the DP camp in Berlin as fast as I could to report to the officials what had happened so that they could try and help save the people that had been taken away. I found a little countryside train station, where I boarded the train. At the first town, I transferred to a train that would take me to Berlin. When I arrived in Berlin, there was already news from Stettin waiting for me. They knew what had happened and also knew where the people had been taken. They told me to get some rest because soon they would have a new mission for me.

CHAPTER **18**:

New Beginnings

I was now living in Berlin and feeling free as a bird for the first time in years. Berlin still looked like a battlefield, nothing but ruins, but there was no more shooting. A few nightclubs had opened in the American sector, and that is where I spent my evenings, sometimes accompanied by a beautiful Fraulein. Life was good then, and I was definitely trying to live it up. I had made many American friends as well. I carried on like this, enjoying life and liberty for about three months.

One night, in one of the nightclubs, I saw a girl performing an acrobatic dance. The minute I saw her, I was fascinated; a tingling sensation went through my body. After her performance, I walked into her dressing room and asked if she would dance with me. She told me she would love to, as long as her mother would permit it. This was not a bad start because I always had good luck with mothers. She pointed out her mother, who was sitting alone at a table. She was a tall and dark woman. I walked over to her and asked her if I could dance with her daughter. She looked me up and down and asked me where I came from since I did not look German. I started telling her my story, and by the time I finished, the club was closing, so there was no more time for a dance. She told me that she was also Jewish and that she had been lucky to survive the Nazi regime with Gentile papers, and now her daughter was trying to earn a living for both of them by dancing. When her daughter came out of the dressing room ready to go home, the mother formally introduced me to her and told her my story in short. The girl's name was Hilda. I found her so attractive that

I was tongue-tied. When they left, I followed them, exchanging a few words every now and then. I accompanied them onto a bus, transferred onto a subway, and then changed to a streetcar until we arrived at their house. Hilda's mother asked me if I would like to come in, but I turned down the invitation as I was already tired. I asked them if it would be okay to come the next day for lunch and that I would be pleased to bring food with me. This was a tempting offer because, at that time, food was a valuable commodity and hard to come by. Hilda gladly accepted the offer.

The following afternoon, I arrived at Hilda's house with a bag of food and rang the doorbell. The door opened, and there was Hilda. I felt as though I had been struck by lightning. She was even more beautiful than I remembered her from the night before. She was not too tall and not too short and had long dark hair and stunning, large black eyes. I stood there and stared at her until she invited me in. I walked in and, frankly, did not understand a word they were saying because all I could hear were bells ringing. While Hilda's mother prepared lunch, Hilda showed me all her pictures from the theater where she used to dance. I asked her if I could have one picture, and she told me to pick one. I picked my favorite one of the bunch and still have that picture to this day. A man could never forget a beautiful girl like her. Not only was she was beautiful, but Hilda was full of love and kindness. We sat down to eat the wonderful lunch Hilda's mother had put together with all the goodies I had brought. We sat at the table for about an hour and a half, eating, looking at each other, and enjoying the food and the company.

When we finished eating, Hilda asked me if I wanted to join her for a walk. I gladly accepted. With her mother's permission, we were on our way. We strolled through Berlin's long and wide streets until we arrived at a park that had been destroyed by bombs and fire. We sat down and began to talk. Hilda was the one asking most of the questions, and I answered. She wanted to know everything about me. I also asked her about her life, but she did not have much to tell me because she was a little girl when the war broke out. All she remembered doing during the war was dancing for food.

After all this chitchat, Hilda asked me if I had ever kissed a girl. I replied honestly that I had. She confided in me that she had never been kissed by a man. Of course, I did not wait any longer and kissed her on the lips. I kissed her so many times that I do not even remember when I stopped. We spent the entire afternoon with our lips locked to one another's. Although neither of us wanted to return home, it was getting dark, and we knew her mother would worry.

As soon as we arrived at her house, Hilda immediately asked her mother if she could go out with me that evening because she had the night off from work. Her mother was kind enough to permit it, and again, Hilda and I went out into the night. We walked and walked. I still remember how there was not much communication between us other than a feeling of togetherness. We were both searching for something we had lost in the war. The remains of the war surrounded us. There were miles and miles of ruins. We were two young people, among the destruction, who had survived so many terrible events caused by the war. We were simply glad to be alive no matter how desolate everything was around us then. We noticed the birds singing and the flowers sprouting on the big heaps of rubble that had once been houses.

We arrived at a small nightclub in the basement of a bombed house. There was a band of five musicians playing beautiful music. I finally got my dance with Hilda. She clung to me and put her head on my shoulder. We danced like this for the rest of the night. I do not think I had ever seen someone as happy as Hilda was that night. We returned to her house early the next morning. Hilda's mother was waiting for us. We talked a little longer at the door and then I kissed her goodnight. From that moment on, I was with Hilda day and night. After some time, Hilda's mother invited me to move in with them, and I was thrilled to accept the offer. Life was wonderful with both Hilda and her mother.

One day, I received a message that said if I still cared for my friends and a few others who had survived the war, I should immediately report to the address on the note. Hilda and her mother noticed right away that something was wrong. They both cried, kissed me, and begged me not to go. They felt that if I left them now, I would never come back. It was hard to leave them both, but I knew I had to help the others in need. I kissed them and walked out of the house. I still remember Hilda waving as I was walking down the street. I did not take my eyes off her, and with every step I took, she became smaller and smaller until I could not see her anymore.

I arrived at the address I was given in the message. Five men were already waiting for me there. We shook hands and began to talk.

They offered me the one job I hated the most. I did not want to go through it again, but knew I had to. There were about fifty young boys who were ready to go to Israel and join the Jewish forces, but they did not have any money or papers to take a single step. I turned to the eldest man and asked him why he had picked me for this mission and why he was sure I could help, especially because I had no money or transportation. He explained that he had been to Stettin and heard about what I had done before, that I could drive anything with wheels, and that I would find a way to help the boys.

There were few cars on the streets that I could steal. I could not steal a truck from the American, British, or French forces because that would be like stealing from our own pocket. I remember meeting a young German boy a few weeks prior, who claimed to be half-Jewish. He had told me that he knew of a garage in the area where a few German cars were parked that no one had yet discovered. I immediately took one man with me to search for him. I knew that the fastest way to find him would be to go back to Hilda and her mother and ask them, but I did not want to do that to them. To have to say goodbye to me one more time would be heartbreaking. I would have to find him on my own. We walked all day, visiting every place I could remember seeing him. By three o'clock in the morning, I had given up hope of ever finding him and went into one final nightclub.

Miraculously, that is where I found him.

He immediately recognized me and was happy to see me. I joined him at his table, and he offered me a drink. All I knew about him was that his name was Bruno. After a few drinks, I asked him if he was still interested in helping the Jewish people, and he answered, "Yes, my friend Bruno is always ready to help!" It took us about two hours to return to where the other men were waiting. The other men started questioning him, and he could not understand a word. Bruno demanded to talk to me only, which pleased me because the others did not speak German and did not know how to approach him properly. I told the men that Bruno and I would return the next day. Once we got outside, Bruno invited me to stay at his place for a good night's rest.

I accepted his offer. The following day I would be able to explain to him in detail what all of this was about. Bruno lived in Tempelhof, about twelve blocks from where we were. We slept until approximately six o'clock in the evening. Bruno prepared something for us to eat, and we began to talk. I asked him if he remembered the location of the German vehicles and then told him why we would need the cars. I explained to him the entire operation, including where we would have to go to pick up the boys. Bruno was excited about the mission and wanted to start immediately. I told him we would need several cars and good drivers, but Bruno did not trust anyone, so we decided that only the two of us would drive. Bruno and I headed out to where he had seen the cars. It was an abandoned building destroyed by the war. I peeked through an opening in the rubble and saw a garage containing some cars but could not tell how many or what condition they were in. We delayed further investigation until the following day when we could bring everybody along to dig out the cars.

The next day, we returned to this building with our men. We dug up the rubble until we made an opening wide enough to get through. I was the first to crawl into the garage to check out the condition of the cars. There were ten cars, but most of them were damaged. I decided that while Bruno and I would start working on two of the cars, the other guys should keep moving the rubble away from the driveway to clear an exit for us. It was a lot of hard work. We were able to get the motors running but could not drive the cars anywhere because all the tires were flat. At this point, we were stuck because there was nowhere to buy tires, and the only cars in the area that we could steal from them were American or British. We had no other option, so I tried to convince myself that it was like taking something that already belonged to us. We successfully stole the tires, and the cars were ready to go. As I took one of the cars for a test drive, an MP stopped me. I was not sure why they had stopped me, but I knew I was driving a car that did not belong to me and had stolen tires. I did not want to take any chances, so I took off. We lost the MPs after a few blocks and returned to the garage. We now had a different problem. The other men wanted to abort the mission because they were not confident that we could successfully make the long trip without having papers to show the authorities.

Bruno and I were not about to give up. Because I spoke fluent Russian and Bruno spoke English very well, I made up two sets of plates and papers, one American and one Russian. Throughout the trip, when we rode through the Russian sector, we put on the American plates, and when we rode through the American sector, we changed them to the Russian plates. This worked out well but slowed us down because we could only use one car since we had to ride together. I was the driver in the American sector, and in the Russian sector, Bruno drove. Even though everything was running smoothly, we still had a huge obstacle ahead of us. We were still quite worried about how we would cross the border to West Germany. When we reached the border, I walked to the guard, a little Russian from Siberia, who began to talk business. I told him the entire story of the Jewish people and how much they now wanted to go to their own country. To my surprise, he listened and assured me that I would not have any problems crossing the border as long as he was on duty. I promised to bring him a wristwatch. Now that I knew we had the border situation under control, we headed back to pick up the men we had to transport to Hamburg.

CHAPTER 19.

To the Rescue

The men were anxiously waiting for us. Unfortunately, we only had room in the car for five people, and because they all desperately wanted to get to Israel, a fight broke out. Bruno and I did not get involved and just sat in the car as seven men piled in after us. We were now on our way to Hamburg. The car was so crowded that I could barely control it, but I did not mind because it was nice and warm. I felt proud of how far we had gotten; after all, I was the one who devised this plan. Even though I was confident, I was still worried about getting to the border. Suddenly, I realized that in all of the confusion before heading out on this mission, I forgot to bring extra gasoline. This was a huge problem because there were no gas stations around.

The car stopped in the middle of the Autobahn, about one hundred and fifty kilometers from Berlin. We were completely stuck. All we could do was wait without knowing for what or whom. It was now the middle of the night, so we all fell asleep. I woke up at about five o'clock in the morning to see nothing but snow everywhere, including all around the car. I could not even open the car door. I rolled down the window and dug my way out, little by little. Bruno crawled out after me. At this moment, we completely forgot about the mission and focused on how we would survive. It was bitterly cold outside, and we all were freezing to death. I kept rubbing my feet to circulate the blood so I would not lose my feet. When I tried to put my boots on again, they did not fit because they were frozen solid. The same thing happened to two other men. I found some rags in the car and wrapped them around my feet. There were not enough rags for everyone, but we all decided that I would use them to look for a solution to our predicament while the others stayed in the car.

By now, it was eight o'clock in the morning, and not one car had passed. Our only hope was for one single car to come our way. Finally, I heard some engine noises coming from a distance. As the sound became louder and louder, I noticed a caravan of trucks approaching us. I quickly jumped into the middle of the road to stop the trucks. Luckily, the first truck was a jeep driven by an American officer. The officer kindly greeted me, and Bruno came running to help with his English. He explained to the officer that we were DPs (displaced persons) on a mission to West Germany and had gotten stuck without gasoline. The officer did not waste a minute; he gave us gasoline and helped us pull the car out of the snow. We had to push it to get it started, and once we got the motor running, we parted in different directions. The American went to the East, and we headed to the West.

We were about fifty miles to the border. The car moved slowly because the snow was piled up high on the road. I stopped the car about two miles from the border and told the other men to wait for me because I wanted to walk to the border to check if my Russian friend was on duty. I walked for about half an hour in deep snow until I reached the post. A Russian guard appeared immediately and asked to see my documentation. I explained to him that I did not want to cross the border; I was looking to see if my friend Sasha was working. He told me that Sasha was scheduled to work first thing in the morning. This would be a huge problem because we would all have frozen to death by then.

I knew we could not wait until morning, and I had to do something now. I asked the Russian if I could come into the guardhouse to warm up a little bit. He allowed me to walk in with him. He offered me a glass of Vodka, more like a tumbler, which I could not refuse, especially now. I took the glass and gently poured the Vodka down my throat. My entire body gradually came back to life. The warmth traveled slowly from head to toe, and I felt better. I could think clearly again. He asked me how I knew Sasha, and I told him I had passed through the border a few weeks ago. Sasha asked me if I could buy him a wristwatch. I explained I had the watch with me and wanted to give it to him. I knew very well that Russian men were crazy about watches; it was an obsession for them. He asked to see the watch and looked at it at least a hundred times. I could tell that he did not want to part with this watch, so I jumped at the opportunity. I told him that if he liked that watch, I would also be pleased to get him one. He was thrilled. I then told him he could keep that watch and I would get Sasha another one; however, I would have to go to Hamburg to do so.

He asked me what I was waiting for and told me to hurry and cross the border now to go into Hamburg. I explained to him that it was not so easy because my friends were waiting for me in their car a few kilometers away, and if I were to go, they would have to come with me because we always traveled together. He said that it would not be a problem for me to cross with my friends. He even offered me a ride to the car. It took us about twenty minutes, and we were on the other side of the border in West Germany. We came to a halt here again, but it was a joyful stop this time. We were so relieved; we did not care what would happen to us. We all got out of the car half frozen, and without asking for permission, we entered the barracks. No one paid any attention to us or to what we were doing. It was as if we were one of them. Bruno went around to look for food and hot coffee. After about twenty minutes, we were on friendly terms with everyone in the barracks. We rested, ate, drank, warmed up, and refreshed ourselves. Then we were on our way again to Hamburg.

Unfortunately, getting to Hamburg was not going to be as easy as we had expected. After driving about fifty kilometers, we encountered another patrol of German police and American MPs. As we did not have any papers, they made us pull over to the side of the road and abandon our car. It all happened so fast that there was no time for any of my tricks. They ordered us into their car and drove us to the next post, where their

110

commanding officer was supposedly stationed. On the way, I came up with an idea. I had to devise some excuse for the commanding officer, so I quickly pulled out the paper I had that was written in Hebrew and that I had used on the Russians while traveling from Germany to Poland. As soon as we arrived at the command post, everyone complained about being hungry and cold. They immediately sent us to a heated room and gave us food. As usual, I was the one who did all the talking; therefore, everyone's attention fell on me. When the officer of the department arrived, the guard called me out first. A very tall man, who was a high-ranking officer, confronted me. He asked me for my name, and of course, I responded, but after that, I could not understand a word of what he said.

They asked me if I spoke German, and I told them I did not. I could not speak English, but to show them that I was willing to cooperate, I pulled the paper with Hebrew writing from my pocket and handed it to the officer. Like all the officers before him, he examined the paper, even turned it upside down, but could not figure it out. I tried to help him by saying the only word in English I knew at that time, which was "Jewish." He then began to understand. After the officer realized the letter was written in Hebrew, he called for a Jewish person in his department. We waited for about two hours for the man to arrive.

When I saw him, I immediately noticed he was an American army chaplain. He asked me if we all were Jewish and then continued with the investigation. He then brought up the subject of the paper written in Hebrew and asked me why I had tried to fool the American officer with it. I was so ashamed that I could not even look at him in his face. I sobbed like a child. When the others saw me cry, they all joined in. Shame was not the only reason I was crying. All that came to my mind was everything I had gone through to prepare for this trip and all the trouble we had been through. I could not believe we had almost made it and now felt trapped and helpless. After the chaplain listened to our entire story, he went out to confer with the other officer. We did not see him again until the next morning. At around nine o'clock the next morning, the chaplain returned with the officer and a few more people dressed in civilian clothing.

They all sat down at a long table. I was scared because it looked like we were in court again, just as we had experienced with the Russian tribunal. We asked questions but did not receive any answers. As always, I was the first to be called. The chaplain wanted to know everything about me starting from the day I was born. We all went through the same routine. It took the entire day for the questioning, and then all the men left, except for the chaplain. We were served food and drinks, and then the chaplain sat down and started telling us a story. He explained that he had inquired about us at the DP camp, and they confirmed who we were and our mission. They also asked the chaplain to give us all the help he could. We were so relieved. We were finally free again but would have to wait until the following morning to get our papers.

The next morning, the chaplain entered our room with a huge smile on his face. He had brought with him new I.D. cards for everyone and explained that we were free to travel all over Germany. I then asked him about the car. The chaplain smiled again and pulled out a special document for the car. We were finally completely free and able to move on. This was a happy day for all of us.

CHAPTER 20:

The Next Chapter

I tried not to waste more time, so we thanked the chaplain and headed to Hamburg. After several hours of driving, we arrived at our destination. I had a letter with me that was addressed to some people in Hamburg. We found them and handed them the letter. These people had been expecting us for several weeks and immediately invited us into their house. There was dinner waiting for us. We cleaned up and sat down for a delicious dinner. We were exhausted, and after everything we had been through, we all went to bed right after dinner. Late the next morning, the lady of the house came to my room with two men. She indicated it was okay for me to talk to them freely. These two men were Greek sailors who spoke a little German so we could communicate. They told me their boat was leaving for Greece the next day, and they could take our boys to Israel, but it would cost one hundred dollars each. This proposition caught me off guard, but the lady interrupted our conversation and closed the deal.

After the men left, the lady properly introduced herself to me. Her name was Lady Anna Minz. She explained to me that she was on a special assignment to locate ships that will take our people to Israel. Her entire family, including her husband, two sons, and brother, had already migrated to Israel. The following morning, we took our boys to the boats and said our goodbyes. Although everyone was so happy that we had reached our goal, it was bittersweet because we did not want to say goodbye. The boat slowly moved out, and they were on their way to the promised land.

Bruno and I went back to the house to prepare everything for our return to Berlin the following morning. Lady Anna served us dinner once again. We woke up early hoping to make it back to Berlin in one day.

We ate a wonderful breakfast, said a warm goodbye to Lady Anna, and were on our way. We took the Autobahn and made it through the American border control without any problems. This time, we did not have to use any tricks. As we headed to the Russian border control, I hoped that my friend Sasha was not there so I would not have to explain what happened to the watch. As usual, luck was not on my side. When we arrived, I saw Sasha standing there. When he saw me, I noticed a smile on his face. He immediately came up to me and apologized, which was odd because I should have been the one making the apologies. I did not know why he was sorry, but I will say it was a wonderful surprise. I promised to bring him a watch next time and see that he would get it. Sasha came up with an idea. He said that if he would not be on duty when I returned, he would tell all the other guards not to give me any trouble so that I could give him the watch upon my return. After sharing a glass of Vodka with Sasha, we continued to Berlin. It took us five hours to reach Potsdamer control, which had always been easy to pass and was no problem. We arrived at Berlin at approximately ten o'clock in the evening and drove straight to the DP camp in Schlachtensee.

Everyone showed up to congratulate us on our successful mission. We had a wonderful celebration that evening. I had a few drinks and left to spend the night in one of my friend's rooms at the camp. I could not sleep. After a while, Bruno came to check on me because he could not sleep as well. We stayed up and talked about what we had experienced and what we may encounter on our next trip. Bruno said that we should stay in his house instead of the DP camp because it would be safer if anyone tried to find me. I told him we would head to his house in the morning.

We left the DP camp the next morning and headed directly to Bruno's house. His mother welcomed me and immediately made me feel right at home. Bruno and I shared a room. We worked together to fix up the room nicely, and once we were finished, his mother had a delicious dinner waiting for us. I felt comfortable in that room and knew I wanted to stay there for a while. Initially, it was wonderful living without any burdens, being lazy, and waiting for the next day without any specific plans.

After two weeks of living like that, I became extremely bored. I decided to go out and look for some action. Bruno accompanied me. We walked all over Berlin, in all the sectors, including the American, British, French, and Russian ones. My goal was to find some food for home and some to sell or barter for other valuable items. Of course, we ran into some minor trouble, especially in the Russian sector, but I always managed to get us out of the trouble just as easily as I managed to get us into it.

One evening, Bruno surprised me. He told me that he had set up a double date for us. Even though I did not like that it was a blind date, I did not have a problem with it. We both dressed up in our best clothes for the date. Because it was a special occasion, we thought we should use our car. This was the first time we had driven it since our trip to West Germany . Bruno and I lived in the American sector but had to drive to the British sector to pick up the girls. It did not take long to get to Kurfürstendamm, the most popular street in Germany, where the best nightclubs and theaters were. We arrived at Café Vien, and the girls were already waiting for us. Two girls sat at a table, and one had her back facing me. I parked my car, and we started to walk toward them. Suddenly, I felt weird in the pit of my stomach, and I started to tremble. When I got closer to the table, without knowing it was her, I cried out, "Hilda," and sure enough, one of the girls turned around. I could not believe it was her. Hilda immediately got up and started to walk toward me. We did not say a word and embraced. We did not want to let go. I do not remember how long we stayed there frozen in each other's arms, but by the time we looked around, about fifty people were staring at us. We decided to go somewhere else. While we were driving, looking for another place, Hilda came up with a great idea. She told me that her mother would be thrilled to see me and that we all should go to her house. We turned the car around and headed to Hilda's house because it was a few minutes away. Hilda entered the house first to break the news to her mother so she would not be too surprised. Immediately, both of them came out of the house. Hilda's mother was crying like a baby and kissed me like she had found her lost child. We all went into Hilda's house, and her mother began to prepare dinner for us.

We ate great food, drank delicious wine, and even had the opportunity to dance to some pleasant music on the radio. It was a real party. Hilda put her beautiful head on my shoulder and whispered, "I love you; I love you." Hilda's kisses were the sweetest kisses I had ever experienced. At the end of the evening, Hilda's mother proposed a toast, wishing that Hilda and I would get engaged. I did not object to it; quite the contrary, I thought the idea was wonderful. And so that evening, Hilda and I became engaged.

After Bruno and his date left, I stayed with Hilda and her mother. They already considered me family and to be the man of the house. Three months later, Hilda and I were married. It was a small ceremony. We did not have a reception or a honeymoon because, unfortunately, we could not afford to, but we were extremely happy. Hilda told me that our love for one another was the most important thing to her. This is how I started married life.

Everything was great for the first few months; it was all love, love, and more love. Then the trouble started. Times started to change, and the value of our dollar grew. Every day, there were new things in stores, and people dressed much nicer. Hilda demanded things from me, but unfortunately, I did not have the money to buy her what she wanted. At that time, even though the value of the dollar had increased, there were still not a lot of jobs available except for cleaning up all the ruins in Berlin. The pay for this kind of work was not enough to live on. I tried to start a business but did not have much luck. After about a year of being unable to give Hilda what she wanted, I decided it would be best to get divorced, and so we did. Even though it was hard for both of us because we loved one another very much, we no longer understood each other. We both knew in our hearts that it would never work out.

Realizing that things were not going great for me and that I had to make a new start, I decided to migrate to the United States. As I boarded the boat that would take me to the Western world, I took one last look at Germany. All the hurt, pain, loss, and pure tragedy was now behind me.

New days of hope, dreams, and liberty were just around the corner.

AFTERWORD

By Liz Becker

Despite enduring a harrowing past and the heartbreaking loss of his entire immediate family, my father persisted in forging a new life. Following the war, he made the journey to the United States. His first wife, Hannah, blessed him with two children, Sheba and Harvey, while his second wife, Betti, brought me, Liz, into the world. Among the joys of his extended family were three cherished grandchildren: Eden, David, and Mikel, and as of 2024, 11 great-grandchildren. Through his unwavering strength, courage, determination, and resilience, my father provided each of us with the opportunity to embrace life.

One of the most impactful memories I cherish dates back to my early teenage years, around 14, during a trip to New York with my parents for a fundraising event centered around the construction of a Holocaust memorial. Standing beside my father, a remarkable encounter unfolded when a man approached him, greeting him with a very warm and long embrace. Upon introduction, he asked if my father had ever shared the tale of helping a young boy swimming across a river. Instantly, I recalled my father telling me a story of crossing a river while fleeing from Nazis. Almost reaching safety, he heard cries and turned to see a young boy, probably around 6 or 7 years old, only halfway across, too weak to swim any further. Without hesitation, my father swam back to guide him to safety, away from the threat of the Nazis. I affirmed to the man that my father had indeed shared that story. To my astonishment, he crouched to my level, locked eyes with mine, and revealed that he was that very boy and that my father had saved his life. I never looked at my father the same after that pivotal day. That was the moment I realized that he was not just a Holocaust survivor, he was a true hero.

Regrettably, my hero, Robert "Bolek" Becker passed away on October 21, 2012, before having the chance to share his extraordinary story with the world. To truly capture his impact on all of us, I will conclude with the eulogy I delivered at his funeral.

My father truly meant the world to me. He was a survivor, a warrior, a protector, and a nurturer. He was a true Neshama who cared deeply for all those around him. As a Holocaust survivor, he believed giving up was never an option and always knew how to overcome any struggle. Even after experiencing such horror, losing his mother, father, grandparents, and siblings, he never lost faith in God.

My dad was definitely one of a kind. Many of us knew him as Cowboy Bob, who had a greater presence than any president. Whenever he walked into a room, all eyes were on him. He would immediately be noticed and heard. He always loved to put smiles on faces and warm hearts with his goodness.

There is so much I have learned from my father, and it would take me hours to list them all, so I will focus on what I feel is the most important.

Dedication: He always finished what he started and did it wholeheartedly.

Loyalty: He was 100% loyal to his family and friends and protected them like no other.

Honesty: I never caught him telling one lie. He was true to others just as he was true to himself.

Respect: He always gave it to those who deserved it and earned it every day of his life for simply being the man he was.

Honor: He honored those who he learned from and cared for. He was a man of his word that fulfilled each and every promise he made. And as I stand here today, I can confidently say that everyone who crossed my father's path honored him.

Value: He knew the value of what was important in life and never needed or yearned for too much.

Strength: He was the epitome of strength. Throughout my life, I have always been able to cope with hardships more easily than others because of the strength given to me by my father's example. Every trial and tribulation, no matter how small or large, always seemed meaningless compared to what my father went through as a teenager. So, when I needed strength, all I would have to do was say to myself if my father overcame what he did, this would be a breeze!

And the most valuable lesson I learned from my father is how to love. Ever since I was a baby, there was not one day that passed without my father telling me he loved me, even up until his passing. Not only did that give me the true confidence that no matter what my future would hold, I was always loved, but it also gave me the ability to tell those I cared for that I loved them easily. That is why now, I will not let one day pass without telling my son I love him, and I know in my heart that he will do the same with his children.

To me, the definition of love is admiration. I truly admire my father and thank God every day for every moment I had with him.

I know he is here with us today, and there is one thing that I did not have time to tell him before his passing, so I would like to do so now.

Daddy, I promise to continue your legacy of strength and honor and take the best care possible of your wife, children, grandchildren, and great-grandchildren. So please rest in peace knowing you have been, and always will be, very present in our lives.

I will miss him dearly and know in my heart that he is smiling down at us, knowing he has again gained his strength to protect and help us all.

ROBERT "BOLEK" BECKER

1924 — 2012

BELOVED HUSBAND
FATHER AND GRANDFATHER

HE WAS THE HEROIC STORY OF
THE JEWISH PEOPLE IN THE
20TH CENTURY. A SURVIVOR,
WARRIOR AND PROTECTOR.
THE LEGACY HE LEAVES SERVES
AS INSPIRATION TO US ALL.

ת' נ' צ' ב' ה'

OTHER PICTURES

BECKER IN UNIFORM (year unknown)

BECKER ON LEFT (others unknown)

Printed in Great Britain
by Amazon

53948475R10076